EARTHQUAKE CLAIMS

TRADE SECRETS

YOU MUST KNOW

TO GET WHAT YOU PAID FOR
FROM YOUR
INSURANCE POLICY

TRAVIS GUNN

A CrossFire Book
Dallas • Denver

To Ron: ALWAYS STICK TO YOUR GUNN'S

Travis Gunn

EARTHQUAKE CLAIMS

TRADE SECRETS
YOU MUST KNOW
TO GET WHAT YOU PAID FOR
FROM YOUR
INSURANCE POLICY

CrossFire Publishing

P.O. Box 1209, Monument, CO 80132

Printed in the United States of America.

Cover design by Rick Carnes

Cover photograph by J. Bear Baker

Library of Congress Catalog Card Number: 94-62148

ISBN: 1-885518-00-5

1 3 5 7 9 10 8 6 4 2

CONTENTS

ABOUT THE AUTHOR

Former Director of Claims for three major insurance companies, and former member of the NAII Executive Claims Council, **Travis Gunn** has trained hundreds of adjusters and supervised the handling of thousands of claims throughout his twenty year career. He is the author of *Hurricane Claims: Trade Secrets You Must Know To Get What You Paid For From Your Insurance Policy* and *Tornado, Wind and Hail Claims: Trade Secrets You Must Know To Get What You Paid For From Your Insurance Policy*. He has personally assisted victims of disasters such as Hurricane Hugo, Hurricane Andrew and the 1994 Earthquake in Los Angeles.

"If you've ever lost at anything because you didn't understand the rules of the game, you'll know why the information contained in this book is priceless." —*Travis Gunn*

To the victims and families of the 1994 Earthquake in Northridge, California.

And to those few brave souls in the insurance business who wished to remain anonymous, I couldn't have done it without you. Remember,
"the truth will set you free."

Using THIS BOOK

Whether you are making a claim for the first time, experienced at making claims, or are thinking about reopening the claim for which you have already been paid, this book will be invaluable to you. Based on my twenty years of personal claims experience, I have included the most effective strategies I have used and had others use effectively on me.

I did my best to give you useful, up to date information. Still, the laws and policies change and are subject to different interpretations. This book does not attempt to replace the need for professional services of any kind. If you want or need legal advice, please seek the services of an attorney.

I am not a contractor or an engineer. Advice on any technical aspect of a structure, repair procedure or material price should be obtained from professionals in those trades.

The claim strategies mentioned throughout this book can be used on both homeowner and commercial claims. Since the commercial or business claim probably will contain issues not common to the average homeowners claim, I have covered these issues more extensively in the business loss edition.

MOST COMMONLY ASKED QUESTIONS ABOUT INSURANCE CLAIMS

Q. How does the insurance company decide what is a fair amount for my claim?

A. From a practical standpoint, the company will pay what you are willing to accept if that figure meets its idea of a "reasonable settlement." Here's the catch—a reasonable settlement to the insurance company depends upon the company's claim department payment philosophy. The company can be so tight it squeaks, or it can be liberal enough to keep the customer satisfied.

There is no magic dollar amount. No magic formula. You just need to know that a claim settlement is totally negotiable!

Q. What if I don't agree with the adjuster on the amount of repairs?

A. Normally you will want to get a contractor's estimate and opinion before the adjuster inspects your property to prevent direct confrontation between you and the adjuster on the repair figures. But if you disagree with the adjuster's estimate, the options from this point are: negotiate, write complaint letters to the insurance company management, get help from your agent, or get help from the State Insurance Department.

Also, most policies provide procedures for "agreeing to disagree." This is known as the "Appraisal Clause." Appraisal is generally the last resort—because the outcome is unpredictable and final! See the chapter, "The Appraisal Clause" for more information.

Q. Will my insurance company cancel my policy if I don't agree with the settlement offer?

A. No. Generally cancellations are the result of a permanent physical change of your property (it burns down or is demolished). Sometimes an insurance company decides it will no longer issue policies in your state or insure your type of property. And, cancellation procedures are on file with your State's Insurance Department and insurance companies must follow these procedures. So don't be afraid to disagree with the settlement offer!

Q. What if my insurance company goes bankrupt?

A. Insurance companies pay special taxes. The State pools the tax dollars into a "guarantee fund." If your company goes bankrupt, you should get your claim paid through the coordination of your State Insurance Commissioner. Contact your State Insurance Department for further information on the guarantee fund if and when it becomes necessary.

Q. What about food and lodging expense for my family while my home is unlivable and while it is being repaired?

A. Most homeowner type policies cover this expense if it is an *additional* expense. See the definition of "additional" and the examples in the chapter, "Is Your Home Unlivable?"

Q. Can I get an advance on my claim while I am waiting to settle?

A. While the policy doesn't exactly provide for it, most insurance companies will issue advance payments—*if asked*. SO ASK!

Note: Some insurance agents have authority to make advance payments without waiting for the claim department to handle the claim.

Q. What is a public adjuster and should I consider hiring one?

A.   A public adjuster offers to handle your insurance claim for a fee. The fee is usually 10% of the total claim, but that's negotiable. Be cautious if the public adjuster cannot provide references and documented credentials showing past insurance company employment.   Inexperienced or non-technically proficient public adjusters may actually delay or complicate the claim (but still collect a fee).   Before signing a contract with a public adjuster, review his or her resume, license and references.

Q. How do insurance adjusters figure out the price of repairs?

A.   Most insurance companies prepare "price guides" that are supposed to reflect the local material, labor, and flat fee prices for a variety of repairs. But be careful—sometimes the price guides are inaccurate or improperly used. For accurate pricing, you should rely solely on the prices quoted by your contractor.

Q. How do I select a contractor to do the repairs?

A. This may be one of your more difficult tasks. If the disaster is large enough, contractors will swarm in from all over the country, set up temporary shop, do some work—and swarm away. It is hard to know who to trust. Try to get a reference from someone who has had repairs done. Your next best choice is to pick a local contractor who can provide references that you can check.

Q. What if I decide to do the repairs myself?

A. If you are competent, or maybe I should say confident enough to handle your own repairs, you are entitled to do so. There are three issues to consider:

1. **Avoid a "cash out" settlement.** "Cash out" is a method invented by adjusters to give you less than what it would cost if a contractor did the repairs. It is a penalty for doing the work yourself. Do *not* accept less money than it would cost to have a qualified contractor do the work!

2. **Get your mortgage company's approval.** Many mortgage companies require you to get approval from them before handling your own repairs—your claim check for the damage to your home will have the mortgage company's name as an additional payee! If you have a mortgage company, check with it before deciding to do your own repairs. Mortgage companies have been known to keep the settlement money and apply it against the mortgage.

3. **Ask about "Holdback Depreciation."** If your company holds back (doesn't pay the dollar difference between the depreciated value and replacement cost until the repairs are done), you probably will need to hire a contractor before you will receive full payment. See the chapter, "Replacement Cost Coverage and Depreciation" for further explanation regarding holdback.

Q. Can I reopen my claim once I have cashed my insurance check?

A. Probably, if you have not signed a release. Sometimes release wording is on the back of the check. However, the insurance company can disregard the wording on the check if it chooses to do so. It happens all the time. See the chapter, "Reopening Your Closed Claim."

Q. How do I tell the insurance company I need more money for my damage after my claim is closed?

A. This is called a "supplemental" claim payment. A supplemental claim is made for additional costs to repair or replace your property that exceed the original settlement amount. To tell the insurance company you need more money, call first then follow up with a letter. See the chapter, "Reopening Your Closed Claim" for more information.

Q. If I don't know the value of an item of personal property, is there a penalty for guessing?

A. Not really. Many values for items of personal property are established by guessing. The adjuster can guess—and so can you.

Q. If I am accused or suspected of filing a fraudulent claim, what should I do?

A. Stop talking, do not write to the company, keep all your documentation, hire an attorney and follow the attorney's advice.

Q. What if I accept money or a donation from F.E.M.A. or the Red Cross? Will it decrease my settlement?

A. No. You paid a premium for the insurance coverage and the insurance company must pay you the full amount you are entitled to collect.

Q. Can I make a claim for the costs to live elsewhere until I find out whether it is safe to live in my home?

A. If you left your home because you felt it was unsafe, then you may be entitled to "additional living expense" coverage up to the time the property is inspected and found to be structurally safe.

Q. My electricity went out due to downed power lines. Should I rent or should I buy a generator if I want to remain in my home?

A. Many insurance companies pay for generator rental in lieu of "additional living expense" payments. Buying a generator may be the best choice, but be sure to read the information about generators in the power outage section of the chapter, "Collecting For The Damage To Your Personal Property."

Q. How much documentation do I need to prove ownership of something I am claiming that was destroyed, or was stolen by looters ?

A. After a disaster, very few people are asked to prove ownership of the property they claim—but the insurance company is still entitled to ask. If you are asked to provide proof of ownership of an item you are claiming, don't panic. One of the following three ways should be acceptable "proof":

> **BEST**—Provide a receipt, credit card sales slip or cancelled check for the purchase of the item.
>
> **BETTER**—Provide photos, owners manuals, or original packaging of the items.
>
> **GOOD ENOUGH**—Provide a letter, signed by someone who knew you owned the item.

(See the chapter, "Collecting For The Damage To Your Personal Property.")

CHAPTER 1

HOW TO FILE YOUR CLAIM

I LOVE THE INSURANCE CLAIM BUSINESS—but I sincerely doubt you bought this book because you do! There are only two reasons I can possibly imagine why you would buy a book on a subject as *boring* as insurance claims: 1. You want to know how to get paid what you are entitled to collect from your insurance policy, *or,* 2. You work for an insurance company and want to know if I am revealing *all* of your long kept trade secrets.

Either way, it is great you picked up this book! You are owed payment for your claim the same as the insurance company was owed (and received!) your premium. So don't feel guilty about reading this book or making a claim for full entitlement. IT IS YOUR RIGHT!

For too long the public has trusted trained representatives of the insurance company to "adjust" their claims. And until now, insurance claim information has primarily come from one source, the insurance adjuster. Alternatives have been few: either hire an attorney who charges by the hour or takes a percentage of the settlement, or hire a public adjuster who also takes a percentage of the settlement. With those choices, most people decide to rely on the insurance company's adjuster to provide information on what they are entitled to collect and to provide a "fair" settlement.

But don't kid yourself. The primary objective of the insurance company is to make money. The only way it can make money is to CONTROL your claim and *minimize* the amount it pays you for your damages! It is as simple as that.

Thus the reason for this book. A new source of information. The material presented here is the product of over twenty years of personal experience in claims. It reveals highly effective strategies enabling you to "level the playing field" and overcome the insurance company's time tested tactics intended to minimize your claim payment.

Filing a claim is simply the process of preparing and presenting facts and evidence (documentation). Doing that is like squeezing toothpaste out a tube—once you squeeze out your version the way you see it, you can't change it. Always tell the truth, but make sure you present the claim in the light most favorable to *you*. You can bet the adjuster will present the claim in the light most favorable to the insurance company.

Just remember, insurance companies have checks and balance systems in place to prevent overpayment. **YOU ARE THE ONLY CHECKS AND BALANCE SYSTEM TO PREVENT BEING UNDERPAID!**

But, before you can ever get paid you must report your claim to the insurance company. This chapter is a basic outline to follow when you are not sure how to start the claim process. If you are beyond this stage, just use this information as a check list.

Check List For Filing Your Claim

✔**Find your policy.** Your policy is made up of coverage forms (pages). The forms are identified by numbers in the corner of each page. Since each form has different coverage information, you need to be sure you have all the forms.

The first page is called the **DECLARATIONS PAGE**. Listed under the heading: **Forms And Endorsements**, are all the forms that apply to your policy (identified by letters or numbers). If you cannot match all the form numbers listed with the forms provided, contact your agent or the company and request copies of the missing forms. Since some insurance companies, especially the larger ones, write their own policies, it is essential that you and the adjuster READ AND RELY SOLELY ON THE POLICY YOU PURCHASED!

✔**Report the loss.** Call your agent or your company—even if your damage looks minor. If you cannot get through on the telephone, send a FAX.

✔**Preserve the evidence**. Collect and save anything that can prove the cause of the damage or the value of a damaged item.

✔**Document your damage in its worst condition.** If you must clean up your home after the earthquake, take photographs before cleaning. Think of it as an injury—doesn't a wound look worse when it is new and still bleeding?

YOUR STRATEGY
TAKE CLOSE UP PHOTOGRAPHS OF ALL DAMAGED PROPERTY—BEFORE YOU CLEAN.

Take close up photographs (no videos—except for posterity) of all the debris, the damage to your home, other structures, and personal property—before you clean up or throw anything away. Everything looks less damaged from a distance! Take plenty of photographs. Be sure to get two prints of the photographs developed. The adjuster may want a set and probably will pay you for them.

✔ **Arrange for temporary repairs** or other measures to protect your property from further damage. Depending on the severity of the earthquake, you may or may not find a repairer available to help you. Do the best you can. Keep receipts of the work completed by others.

✔ **Arrange for another place to live if your home is unlivable.** (Check the definition for unlivable in the chapter, "Is Your Home Unlivable").

> **Note:** If your Aunt Carole lets you stay at her house for free, there is no additional expense to claim! There must be a receipt or a legitimate charge for this expense to collect under the coverage.

✔ **Return to normal sales/service or production when possible,** if your loss is to your business. Provide documentation (your reasons listed in writing) why you could not return to normal business during the down period.

✔ **Make a list of the damaged property.** Include the date of purchase and *today's* replacement cost for all your damaged personal property. List *everything* that is damaged, despite the value to you personally!

✔ **Keep track of your time and expenses.** The cost of labor for cleanup and temporary repairs is collectable under your policy, even if it is your labor.

Note: The amount you will be paid for your labor is negotiable. Your labor should be valued the same as having the work done by a person in that trade.

✔ **Ask for an advance payment as soon as possible.** The agent, adjuster, or insurance company can help if you need financial assistance immediately.

✔ **Create a file or order the CLAIM SIMPLI-FILER** (to order, see the appendix) to hold all the information and documentation you will be gathering throughout the claim. Write down everything you do and the name of any person with whom you speak. Make sure you note dates and times. This can become *very* valuable information.

✔ **Select a contractor** to write an estimate of your damage.

Special Considerations For Condo Unit Owners Claims

✔ **Get a copy of the by-laws from your association** to confirm who pays for the damage to the interior walls of your unit. The insurance company should abide by the wording in the by-laws. Generally, you are responsible for repairs to interior walls—the association is responsible for repairs to commons areas and exterior walls.

> **Note:** If you bought contents coverage and did not buy coverage for the interior structure, you may be able to get an extension of coverage (usually 10% of your personal property coverage limit) to cover the interior walls, cabinets, carpeting, etc.

For the cost to repair damage to the commons areas that is not covered by insurance, you may get hit with an assessment from your association. The typical insurance policy limits coverage for

17

an assessment to $1,000.00. Your coverage may be higher or unlimited. Have the insurance adjuster or company show you in *your policy* the limit of your assessment coverage.

The Commercial And Business Owners Policy

The insurance claims strategies throughout this book, while geared to home owners, can apply to the commercial and business owners policy as well. I have seen business people—doctors, lawyers, retailers, etc.—experts in their fields, lose thousands of dollars in their insurance settlements. To obtain specific information for business interruption claims, order: *"The Gunn Guide To Business Claims."* (See the appendix.)

YOUR STRATEGY
IF YOU REPORT YOUR CLAIM LATE, WRITE A BRIEF LETTER STATING THE REASON.

Making a late claim just means you didn't turn your claim in when everyone else did (within the first few weeks). All policies have provisions that require prompt notice after a loss, so you will need to explain why you are reporting your claim late. The most common reasons for late reporting are:

- **OUT OF TOWN**

- **SERIOUS ILLNESS**

- **BELIEF THAT THE DAMAGE WAS UNDER THE DEDUCTIBLE**

- **DID NOT SEE THE DAMAGE UNTIL NOW**

You should write the company a letter if you are reporting your claim late. Here is a sample letter:

Sample Letter When You Are Reporting Your Claim Late:

ABC Insurance Company
100 North First Street
Los Angeles, CA. 90090

RE: Insured: Needa Hand   Date: May 29, 199X
     Date of Loss: 01-17-199X
     Policy number: 123-55-98 B
     Claim Number: 456-89-000

Attention: Seefer Uself, (Adjuster or Agent)

Dear Mr. Uself,

(*Amend the following paragraphs to fit your situation*)
As I informed you, I had earthquake damage to my home on January 17, 199X. Since I was not at home at the time it occurred, I had no idea my home was damaged. It wasn't until May 23, 199X that I noticed an uneven surface under my carpet. This prompted me to look at the foundation slab. I called my report of loss into your office on May 24, 199X.

I believe this is reasonable notice of loss under the circumstances. If your company is reserving any right to deny for late notice please notify me in writing within 10 days from the date of this letter.

Very truly yours,

Needa Hand

Making A Claim Without Earthquake Coverage

If you didn't buy earthquake coverage, all may not be lost. If you have a Homeowners policy, some insurance companies will pay for additional living expenses up to two weeks even though there is no earthquake coverage.

You may find coverage for other losses associated with an earthquake such as:

- **FIRE**
- **EXPLOSION**
- **FOOD SPOILAGE**
- **GLASS BREAKAGE**
- **LOOTING (THEFT)**

Don't be afraid to submit a claim. Here is a sample letter to request "Additional Living Expense" coverage if you did not purchase earthquake coverage:

> **Note**: See the chapter, "Is Your Home Unlivable" for more information on Additional Living Expense coverage.

Sample Letter To Request Consideration For "Additional Living Expense" Coverage When You Have No Earthquake Coverage:

ABC Insurance Company
100 North First Street
Los Angeles, CA. 90000

RE: Insured: Wertha Try   Date: January 21, 199X
        Date of Loss: 01-17-199X
        Policy #: 123-55-97 B
        Subject: Additional Living Expense Claim

Attention: Claims Dept., (Company or Agent)

Dear Sirs,

(*Amend the following paragraphs to fit your situation*)
As I informed you, I had earthquake damage to my home on January 17, 199X. I sustained (*power outage, food spoilage, looting, fire, explosion, or glass breakage*) on my premises. I was unable to live at home for (*amount of time*). I waited for a city inspection to verify safety. It wasn't until February 1, 199X that I was able to move back into my home. Enclosed is a promissory note for rent from the people I stayed with during this period.

If your company is reserving any right to deny coverage or if you deny my claim, please provide me with specific reasons for the denial including a copy of the policy, highlighted, that permits the denial. Please notify me in writing of the status of my claim within 10 days from the date of this letter.

Very truly yours,

Wertha Try

CHAPTER 2

YOUR CONTRACTUAL DUTIES AFTER AN EARTHQUAKE

One common way for the insurance company to put you on the defensive is to point out what *you* failed to do on your claim. Beat them to the punch! Meet the contractual duties and you take away an opportunity for the insurance company to use your oversights to its benefit.

All insurance policies contain specific duties you must do after a loss. In most homeowners policies, these "contractual duties" are found in **SECTION I—CONDITIONS**. There are seven (7) primary duties you must comply with to meet your responsibilities under the policy. The seven primary duties are:

1. **Notify the insurance company as soon as practical of a loss.**

If you didn't notify your insurance company immediately after the loss, provide a written explanation why the report of loss was delayed. See the chapter, "How To File A Claim."

2. Keep the loss from getting bigger by protecting your property from further damage.

While you have a duty to protect your property from further damage, most homeowners policies will allow for reimbursement of the expense. Do your best to secure and board up the property to minimize any further damage. Keep track of *your* labor and receipts for expenses—you can get reimbursed.

3. Submit your "Proof of Loss" along with supporting documents within the specified time.

The insurance company will advise you if it requires a proof of loss.

4. If requested, provide additional supporting documents.

Here is an example of providing additional supporting documents: if the building is destroyed, the insurance company has the right to request the original plans and specifications of the building (if available).

5. Exhibit and separate, damaged from undamaged property.

You also must show the insurance company the damaged property as often as reasonable.

6. Produce accounting and other records for examination and permit copies to be made.

This is self explanatory. The insurance company prefers to make copies of the original documents to prevent alterations of bills, receipts, or book entries.

7. **Submit to a statement (examination) under oath.**

A request for a statement under oath always suggests that the insurance company is suspicious of some part of your claim. You may want to consult with an attorney if you are asked to submit to a statement under oath.

> **Note:** Do not confuse a statement under oath with a recorded statement. An adjuster who requests a recorded statement is not always suspicious of your claim—it may just be company procedure.

You are obligated to meet your contractual duties. Always document in your file or **CLAIM SIMPLI-FILER** the times and ways you have complied. (See appendix to order.)

CHAPTER 3

THE KEY PLAYERS

Your damage will be evaluated by you, your contractor, the adjuster and possibly an engineer. As you might guess, that will result in several individual opinions—possibly very different opinions. Your goal is to organize and orchestrate the key players so the individual opinions become a "group" opinion—and you get everything you are entitled to in the process.

KEY PLAYER #1: You

You are more than the victim of an earthquake, you are a key player. The following strategies will help you take an active role in evaluating your claim. They also will arm you with the tactics you must use to avoid being a victim again—at the hands of the insurance company!

YOUR STRATEGY
DON'T BE INTIMIDATED.

It is often said that to the degree we are not intimidated, measures our success. A powerful insurance company, with hard to understand policies, and a pack of lawyers on staff may seem at first like a formidable opponent. But you have more knowledge of your claim than anyone. If you allow the insurance company or any key player to intimidate you—be prepared to accept whatever settlement bone is thrown your way. If the key players believe you are knowledgeable about your claim, you have significantly improved the "level of the playing field."

YOUR STRATEGY
GET SOME RESPECT.

Fact—all people are *not* treated equally by insurance companies. Fact—some people are even *mis-treated* by insurance companies. Believe me when I tell you, don't be a wishy-washy, "anything will do, anytime, anywhere, because I'm desperate," person. As hard as times are, you must maintain composure, maneuver yourself into a position of strength and gain some respect. The other key players must treat you at *least* as an equal key player—not as an uninformed, weak victim. To "get some respect" here are a few ideas:

- **DRESS LIKE A BUSINESS EXECUTIVE** for every meeting with any key player. (You will undoubtedly and intentionally be overdressed—don't be surprised if the adjuster shows up in a tee shirt and jeans!)

- **DO NOT BEGIN COMPROMISING** on what you want or are willing to accept until you get to the final stage of negotiating. (And then don't compromise too much!)

- **SET ALL THE APPOINTMENTS AROUND YOUR SCHEDULE.** Don't compromise your time to meet their schedules.

- **BE SPECIFIC ABOUT WHAT YOU WANT.**

- **ORGANIZE YOUR CLAIM DOCUMENTATION.** Create a file—or use the **CLAIM SIMPLI-FILER.**

YOUR STRATEGY
TIME THE ADJUSTER'S INSPECTION.

Controlling the outcome of the claim starts with effective use of the time before the adjuster arrives. Your goal is to be prepared, at the first meeting with the adjuster, to discuss your claim knowledgeably. Preparation will take a little time. You should first arrange for a contractor to inspect your damage, then arrange the adjuster's inspection of your property accordingly.

Sometimes you cannot avoid meeting with the adjuster before you are prepared. No problem. Advise the adjuster that you intend to have a contractor inspect your property and you will get back with the adjuster as soon as possible.

KEY PLAYER #2: The Contractor

I strongly recommend you obtain the services of a qualified contractor to work with you on your claim—regardless of the size or amount of damage. The contractor is the expert on how the repairs should be made and the cost of doing the repairs. You should not settle your property damage claim without using one.

YOUR STRATEGY
SECURE THE SERVICES OF A QUALIFIED CONTRACTOR.

Choosing your contractor is very important. Choose wisely. One who writes a particularly low estimate trying to be competitive or one who writes an exorbitant estimate—for a fee—may do you more harm than good. Here are a few tips to help you choose a contractor:

TIPS ON CHOOSING A CONTRACTOR

- **OBTAIN A CONTRACTOR WHO KNOWS THE DEPARTMENT OF BUILDING AND SAFETY RESTRICTIONS.** (Ask!)

- **ALWAYS OBTAIN YOUR CONTRACTOR'S LICENSE NUMBER.** (It should be on the business card.)

- **CHECK THE VALIDITY OF YOUR CONTRACTOR'S LICENSE** through the State Contractors Licensing Board. **In California call toll free (800) 321-2752.** Make sure the contractor you are using is licensed under that number.

- **CHECK WITH THE BETTER BUSINESS BUREAU** to see if any complaints have been filed against your contractor.

- **ASK FOR A COPY OF YOUR CONTRACTOR'S LIABILITY AND WORKER'S COMPENSATION INSURANCE POLICIES.**

- **OBTAIN REFERENCES**.

It is *very* important to note—THE CONTRACTOR WHO WRITES THE ESTIMATE DOES *NOT* HAVE TO BE THE ONE WHO DOES THE REPAIRS! And remember, the insurance company is *not* responsible for the work, materials or craftsmanship of the contractor or repair person you select.

YOUR STRATEGY
DON'T MAKE THE DECISION TO DO YOUR OWN REPAIRS UNTIL AFTER YOU HAVE SETTLED YOUR CLAIM.

Until the claim is settled, there is simply no need to make the decision to do your own repairs. Some insurance companies will not want to pay you to do the work at the same rate charged by the contractor. Always get a contractor to give you an estimate of the cost of the repair work, even if you don't hire that person to do the repairs.

YOUR STRATEGY
YOU DON'T NEED MULTIPLE ESTIMATES IF YOU HAVE DECIDED ON A CONTRACTOR.

If you have found the contractor you want to do the repairs, there is no reason to obtain additional bids or estimates. This isn't an auction! If the adjuster wants competitive bids, ask for a copy of that part of the insurance policy requiring competitive bids. I have never seen such a requirement in *any* policy. The adjuster will just have to work out the repair costs with your chosen contractor.

YOUR STRATEGY
MAKE THE INSURANCE COMPANY GUARANTEE—IN WRITING—THE WORK OF ITS CONTRACTOR.

If the adjuster still insists on you obtaining other bids or on using the insurance company's contractor, you are put in the position of believing that you must either use the insurance company's contractor or take the money and pay the difference yourself—if your contractor's estimate is higher.

YOU DO *NOT* HAVE TO USE ONE OF THE INSURANCE COMPANY'S CONTRACTORS. But if you decide to, or you feel you are being forced to, agree *only if* the insurance company willguarantee—in writing—the quality of the work of any of its contractors!

The insurance company really doesn't want to be responsible for a contractor's work, but if the insurance company wants to force a marriage between you and its contractor and is willing to guarantee its contractor's work, the game isn't over yet. You tell that contractor, in person, that you intend to examine his work in detail, and any delays or poor workmanship you find will be dealt with appropriately. It won't take any time at all for that contractor to decide he is probably not interested in working for you or that he cannot do the job at the insurance company's price!

YOUR STRATEGY
REACH AN UNDERSTANDING WITH THE CONTRACTOR.

Be sure to reach an understanding with your contractor on:

1. WHAT WORK NEEDS TO BE DONE. Agree with the contractor what the extent or "scope" of repair is before a bid is completed. If you feel that it is necessary to replace an item instead of repairing or patching it, SAY SO NOW!

2. WHO WILL DO THE WORK. Find out who will be performing the work. Find out their experience levels, how long they have worked for the contractor, their dependability etc. You also will need to know who the subcontractors are to obtain lien waivers (discussed later in this chapter).

3. QUALITY OF MATERIALS TO BE USED. You will want to make sure that the types of materials being used are at least equal to the quality of the materials that were damaged—if not better!

4. WHEN THE WORK WILL BE DONE. After a disaster, contractors may take on more jobs than can be timely completed, so make sure the contractor accurately estimates how long the repairs will take. This is very important if the repairs make your home unlivable—you may be entitled to Additional Living Expense coverage for this period of time!

Go over all the damage and your ground rules (you want something replaced, not repaired, etc.) with the contractor—item by item. If you are satisfied you have a meeting of the minds on the extent of damage, quality of the materials used, and methods of repair, then give the contractor the okay to complete the estimate.

YOUR STRATEGY
HAVE THE CONTRACTOR PROVIDE A DETAILED BREAKDOWN OF THE CHARGES IN THE REPAIR ESTIMATE.

The contractor will know from experience approximately how much he will charge to do the repairs—and he will know *before* the estimate is ever completed. So to save time, it is easier for a contractor to lump the costs of several tasks into one large dollar amount to arrive at the predetermined figure. And nothing infuriates an adjuster more than to work with a contractor's estimate that has little or no detail showing how the contractor arrived at the totals.

The adjuster's job is to chisel away at the contractor's estimate. It is much easier for the adjuster to shave off a few big numbers than it is to chip away at many small numbers. So to keep the adjuster from chiseling away at the repair costs, request that your contractor provide a detailed breakdown of the items to be repaired.

YOUR STRATEGY
BE THERE WHEN THE CONTRACTOR AND THE ADJUSTER GO OVER THE DAMAGE.

Be at the first meeting between the adjuster and your contractor. It is preferable to arrange this meeting when the adjuster makes the first inspection of your damage. Your presence will allow the contractor to speak freely about what repairs *you and he* have decided upon.

YOUR STRATEGY
RELY ON THE CONTRACTOR TO ESTIMATE YOUR DAMAGE—BUT NOT TO SETTLE YOUR CLAIM!

It is always preferable for you to use your contractor's estimate to obtain the accurate prices and procedures to repair your damage. But—YOU SHOULD NOT RELY ON THE CONTRACTOR TO SETTLE YOUR CLAIM! The contractor is not an expert on insurance, so limit the contractor's involvement to *estimating* the damage! There are items of damage (other than contents) that you can make a claim for that your contractor may not be aware of and won't be included in his repair estimate. Estimating the damage is the contractor's role—settling the claim is yours!

YOUR STRATEGY
BEFORE ANY REPAIRS BEGIN, GET A CONTRACT WITH THE CONTRACTOR.

Before a single hammer is raised, make sure you get a contract with your contractor covering (at a minimum):

- **A BASIC AGREEMENT:** Lays out scope of work, method of payment, and completion time.

- **THE GENERAL CONDITIONS:** Outlines everyone's responsibilities—yours, the contractor's, and your architect's or engineer's.

- **THE PLANS AND SPECIFICATIONS:** Tells how the job will be done and lists the quantity and quality (grade) of materials to be used.

- **CHANGES AND MODIFICATIONS:** How to proceed if you change your mind as to what you want the contractor to do.

Your contractor should have a basic contract form. If you don't understand or feel comfortable with the contract, consulting with an attorney may be helpful.

YOUR STRATEGY
OBTAIN "LIEN WAIVERS" FROM ANYONE WHO WILL DO WORK OR SUPPLY MATERIALS TO YOUR PROPERTY.

While this book is about earthquake claims, I believe it necessary to warn you about potential claims that can be made against *your* property. There are contractors who, for whatever reason, do not pay their suppliers or subcontractors. So to protect yourself from a lien (claim) against your property by a subcontractor or supplier who was not paid by your contractor, request a "waiver of liens." Get them from your contractor, his subcontractors, and the suppliers of materials before repairs begin.

> **Note:** If you do not get lien waivers signed, you may want to put all the subcontractors' names on the payment check as additional payees.

KEY PLAYER # 3: The Adjuster

Insurance adjusters come from all over the country after a disaster to adjust claims. Their skill levels vary from no prior experience to highly trained. The larger the disaster—the less picky insurance companies are in selecting adjusters to handle the claims. So just because an adjuster shows up to handle your claim, don't assume that that person is skilled at adjusting claims.

There are two basic types of adjusters: the "staff" and the "independent." Find out which type has been assigned to your claim.

Independent Adjusters

Independent adjusters are not regular employees of the insurance company. They are hired (by contract) only when an insurance company has significantly more claims than its normal staff can handle.

Independent adjusters are motivated to handle your claim by money. BIG money! Independent adjusters earn between $15,000 and $100,000 gross per month following a major disaster. Generally they are paid per claim. So the more claims they close—the more money they make. It doesn't take a rocket scientist to figure out the independent adjuster will be in a big hurry to get through your claim and get on to the next!

Racing through your adjustment at warp speed as they rush toward the cash can result in a sloppily handled claim. Damage gets overlooked, available coverages get overlooked, and errors are made. It is not uncommon to get paid SIGNIFICANTLY LESS than what is owed if the claim is handled too haphazardly. So, make sure the adjuster knows *you* aren't in a big hurry!

YOUR STRATEGY
DON'T PRESSURE AN INDEPENDENT ADJUSTER TO SETTLE YOUR CLAIM TOO QUICKLY.

Higher claim settlements take adjusters more time to calculate. So tell the independent adjuster to TAKE TIME to settle your claim. If you need money quickly, ask for advances.

Staff Adjusters

The staff adjuster is a full time permanent employee of the insurance company. These people don't make $15,000 to $100,000 per month and thus, are not directly motivated by money to quickly close your claim. Their self esteem, salary increases, and promotions are driven by how good they can make their claim files look and by reducing the amounts paid on claims.

Your claim file must "look good" to go through the claim payment process. Documentation is the name of the game with any adjuster but it is particularly important with a staff adjuster. The staff adjuster must have "proof" (documentation) to justify payment of your claim.

YOUR STRATEGY
PROVIDE DOCUMENTATION TO MAKE THE ADJUSTER'S CLAIM FILE "LOOK GOOD."

I cannot stress enough the need to provide "documentation." (See the chapter, "The Secrets To Successful Insurance Claim Negotiations" for a list of examples of documentation.) A well documented file will more likely result in receiving your maximum entitlement. Provide receipts, estimates, quotes—anything possible in writing—to support your claim. It will make it more difficult for any adjuster to be stingy with your claim payment if you have done your homework.

KEY PLAYER #4: The Agent

A good insurance agent can be very valuable to you when you make a claim. Your future business and the future business received by word of mouth referrals is what motivates an insurance agent. Therefore, A GOOD INSURANCE AGENT WILL BE VERY CONCERNED THAT YOU BE TAKEN CARE OF PROPERLY!

Agents have well developed channels of communication within the insurance company. Don't be afraid to make requests for help. The agent can easily relay your message to the insurance company and get your request to the "right" people. Some pressure applied by the agent can get the company to *quickly* respond to your needs.

Most insurance companies authorize their agents to write checks to insureds for advance payments on their claims. If you need an advance, ask your agent first.

KEY PLAYER #5: The Structural or Consulting Engineer

An earthquake causes damage that is difficult to assess. Walls or roof supporting structures can move or shift—and to an untrained observer the structural damage may not be obvious.

If there are new cracks in the walls or any sign the roof, floors, retaining walls, doors or windows may have shifted, have a contractor examine these areas closely. If the contractor believes the building may have structural damage, a consulting or structural engineer may need to be involved in the claim. Here are a few other reasons to involve an engineer in your claim:

<u>USE A STRUCTURAL ENGINEER TO</u>:

- **EVALUATE THE STRUCTURAL SAFETY OF THE PROPERTY**

- **ASSESS THE EXTENT OF DAMAGE**

- **FIGURE OUT IF THE DAMAGE IS REPAIRABLE**

- **HELP THE CONTRACTOR IN DETERMINING HOW BEST TO REPAIR THE DAMAGE**

- **PROVIDE DOCUMENTATION FOR YOU TO USE**

Here is a word of caution: Engineers are not insurance claims experts and some try to get involved in the settlement process by suggesting what you are owed. When you hire one for a specific purpose, make sure you tell the engineer what it is you want inspected and limit his involvement in the settlement process.

> **Note:** Some policies include coverage for engineering reports. Always include the fees of the engineer you used in your claim.

YOUR STRATEGY
BEWARE OF THE "HIRED GUN."

Whether it is the insurance company's contractor or an "expert" engineer, you may be facing a "hired gun" when the *insurance company* calls one of these people out on your claim. The "expert" is eager to pay lip service to the company to continue to get more business. And what does it take to continue to receive the insurance company's business? The "hired gun" must help to save the insurance company money—and on *your* claim! Of course, sending out an engineer at the insurance company's expense is proclaimed a "service to you." Some service! I suggest you rely solely on the opinions of experts *you* hire.

CHAPTER 4

THE SECRETS TO SUCCESSFUL INSURANCE CLAIM NEGOTIATIONS

YOUR STRATEGY
UNLESS THE ADJUSTER IS A REAL JERK,
PLAY IT COOL—FOR NOW.

You may be dealing with the same adjuster for awhile, so you might as well start things off on the right track. Remember the old saying, "You catch more flies with honey..." I'm sure you already know this, but it is easy to forget with the stress following a disaster. Unless the adjuster is a real jerk, or until you can clearly see that the adjuster is not working in your best interest, try to play it cool. Having a harsh or demanding attitude will only make negotiations more difficult.

Adjusters are painfully aware that you can complain and make their jobs miserable. Verbal attacks, rudeness, threats or unreasonable demands to get you what you have coming will only cause the adjuster to document carefully and prepare the claim file as "protection" against your complaints. There may come a time to make a complaint—if and when that time comes, you don't want the adjuster to be prepared for it!

YOUR STRATEGY
DON'T GET PANICKY.

Unless your claim is being denied outright, you will get paid eventually. You simply cannot be desperate or panicky for money and still negotiate effectively. If you need money quickly, request advances.

YOUR STRATEGY
DON'T TAKE IT PERSONALLY.

The earthquake was a traumatic experience for you, but your claim is just business to an adjuster. So try to maintain composure in all negotiations, even if you are offended by what the adjuster offers on your claim.

YOUR STRATEGY
DON'T APPEAR AS THOUGH YOU ARE IN DESPERATE NEED OF MONEY.

Do not assume looking "down and out" and in need of financial help will get you more money. It usually works just the opposite. The adjuster knows a little money means a lot when you don't have much! As with most things in life, the higher settlements tend to go to those people who don't appear to need it, just like banks seem to lend money only to people who can show they don't need it. Wanting what you are fully entitled to collect is a strength—being desperate for it is a weakness.

YOUR STRATEGY
DON'T MAKE EMOTIONAL DECISIONS.

You will have a strong urge for immediate action. Resist it. Don't try to force a hasty settlement in an attempt to "put this all behind you." This is a tough time, but don't make it tougher by making an emotional decision now that you may regret later.

YOUR STRATEGY
NEVER OFFER A BRIBE.

Here is a word of caution. Never give gifts or money to an adjuster. A "kickback" would not only be unethical, but the act could be deemed part of a conspiracy to defraud the insurance company.

YOUR STRATEGY
BE PREPARED TO NEGOTIATE.

The word "negotiations" conjures up different feelings for everyone. For some it is a challenge, for others it is the *last* thing they want to do. If you lack confidence or feel inexperienced, have no fear. Being prepared by doing all your documentation homework can give you the confidence you need to combat the many negotiating tactics adjusters use.

YOUR STRATEGY
DOCUMENT EVERYTHING!!!

Documentation is mentioned in many places in this book because I cannot emphasize enough the need for good documentation. Put everything possible in writing. An expression I use is, "IF IT ISN'T IN YOUR FILE, IT DOESN'T EXIST OR IT DIDN'T HAPPEN!" Use this list for the types of things you should document in your file. Or just follow the complete fill-in-the-blank forms in the **CLAIM SIMPLI-FILER**. Be sure to include names, dates and times. (To order, see the appendix.)

DOCUMENTATION TO INCLUDE IN YOUR FILE:

- **EVERY CONVERSATION** with the adjuster or any insurance company personnel.

- **COPIES OF ANY WRITTEN CORRESPONDENCE.**

- **COPIES OF ALL WRITTEN ESTIMATES.**

- **PHOTOGRAPHS** of all damaged property.

- **ADDITIONAL LIVING EXPENSE DOCUMENTATION.**

- **ANY DOCUMENTS SUPPORTING PROOF OF OWNERSHIP.** (Examples would be receipts and owner's manuals). Only provide this information if the adjuster requests it.

- **ANY TAPE RECORDED CONVERSATIONS.** (See the chapter, "Hardball Negotiation Strategies.")

- **ANYTIME YOU ATTEMPT CONTACT, AND THE RESPONSE YOU RECEIVE.** (The adjuster didn't return a phone call for 7 days, missed or cancelled appointments, etc.)

- **ANYTHING ELSE IN WRITING** that will support your claim.

YOUR STRATEGY
DON'T MAKE LIGHT OF YOUR CLAIM.

Many people get "survivor's guilt" after an earthquake. In an attempt to show compassion for those less fortunate (who have more severe damage) you might want to tell the insurance company or the adjuster to take care of others first. While there is no need to demand to be first in line if your home isn't demolished, there is no reason to offer to be last either.

Your compassion could easily be misinterpreted. The adjuster may believe that *you* think you have a small claim or have low payment expectations. You will be put in non-urgent status, which may put your settlement off until last. If you want to show compassion for those less fortunate, donate your time to charity.

YOUR STRATEGY
PRESENT YOUR CLAIM FOR THE MAXIMUM AMOUNT RECOVERABLE.

Just like taking every tax deduction the IRS allows, you should make claim for all your property damaged in the earthquake. If you decide the 30 year old bird bath that was damaged is of no value to you, list it anyway. Whether your claim is personal property, building damage, or additional living expense, there is nothing wrong with presenting your claim for the maximum amount recoverable as long as you do not lie.

YOUR STRATEGY
DON'T LOOK FOR SPECIAL TREATMENT JUST BECAUSE THIS IS YOUR FIRST CLAIM.

Telling an adjuster "this is the first claim I have ever had" is a waste of your time. You won't be treated any better than someone who has filed twenty claims. In fact, you may put yourself at a disadvantage—the adjuster may have as easier time taking advantage of someone who doesn't know the claims process. (Don't expect special treatment for the number of years you made premium payments on time, either!)

YOUR STRATEGY
DON'T BEGIN GIVING CONCESSIONS OF ANY KIND TOO EARLY IN THE NEGOTIATION PROCESS.

Don't give in too early. The adjuster will not remember any concession you made early in the adjustment process (like that old bird bath you just didn't claim). Claim everything damaged—no matter how slight—and hold your ground until it is time to talk final settlement.

YOUR STRATEGY
BE CLEAR ABOUT WHAT YOU EXPECT.

Don't send the adjuster (or the contractor) on a "scavenger hunt" to find your damage. Be clear about what you think is damaged and what you expect ought to be done about it. If you think your garage needs to be rebuilt, say so. If you think you need a new wall or driveway, new carpet, a new patio cover, or your home is a total loss, say so now—loud and clear. Let the adjuster know up front what it will take to satisfy you, and settle your claim.

YOUR STRATEGY
KNOW THE BUZZ WORDS—SPEAK THE INSURANCE LINGO.

Using key phrases and words can have great impact when talking or negotiating with an adjuster. Using the right words tells the adjuster that you understand the game. In fact, an adjuster may be less likely to overlook something or take advantage of someone who knows the claim process. Here are a few words or statements you may sprinkle into your conversations with the adjuster or insurance company personnel:

- Use the abbreviated term **"A.L.E."** instead of **"Additional Living Expense."** (Only insurance people call it A.L.E.)

- Asking the adjuster about **"holdback depreciation"** will tell the adjuster you are aware of how replacement cost coverage works.

- What two words make any adjuster's hair stand on end? **"BAD FAITH."** When the adjuster or the company refuses to meet their obligations to you, you may have evidence to support a "bad faith" claim. This could result in a lawsuit against the insurance company and an award for many times the amount of the actual claim. But don't use the phrase "bad faith" lightly—save that ammunition for "hardball." See the chapter, "Hardball Negotiation Strategies."

I have tried to use common insurance lingo throughout this book and in all the sample letters I have provided. The index contains many more phrases and definitions you may want to use.

YOUR STRATEGY
DON'T BELIEVE THE EXCUSE THAT THE ADJUSTER DOES NOT CONTROL THE SETTLEMENT AMOUNT.

If the person who is adjusting your claim is a skilled adjuster and a good negotiator, you have probably been made to feel that he or she is on *your* side. A "good adjuster" (the insurance company's definition) builds rapport with you and gains your trust.

You may feel as though you are being treated right—and maybe you are—but if you ask for something you believe you are entitled to which was not included in the adjuster's estimate, and the adjuster squirms out of paying for it by putting the blame on the insurance company, LOOK OUT!

For example (and there are hundreds of examples), you ask for boarding fees for your pet goat under "Additional Living Expense." Wincing, the adjuster says something like, "Gee, I don't think the company will go for that," or, "The company usually doesn't pay for those things." Big, bad insurance company! You reluctantly agree and thank the adjuster for all the effort put forth to "squeeze" your settlement money out of the insurance company. The adjuster then proceeds to write a report noting all the ways money was saved on your settlement (pet boarding—denied, etc.)

The truth is, THE ADJUSTER IS THE INSURANCE COMPANY for all practical and legal purposes! Even if the adjuster is the kindest and most trustworthy person you have ever met, remember, the adjuster works for, is an agent of, and is paid by the insurance company.

> **Note:** If the adjuster verbally "denies" any part of your claim, (like in the previous example) see the chapter, "If Part Of Your Claim Is Denied."

45

YOUR STRATEGY
NEVER ACCEPT THE ADJUSTER'S RESPONSE, "Oh, F.E.M.A. Will Pay For That."

The adjuster should never tell you to get reimbursed for part of your property claim from some other source. This amounts to a partial denial of your claim. If this happens, follow the steps in the chapter, "If Part Of Your Claim Is Denied."

YOUR STRATEGY
DON'T ASSUME THE FIRST OFFER IS THE LAST.

Insurance adjusters regularly make an offer using the lingo: "This amount is what you have coming to you under your policy." If the adjuster uses this expression, your translation should be: "We would like for you to accept this amount, unless of course you have any objections."

YOUR STRATEGY
SMILE AND SAY "NO."

You will be amazed at the effect of smiling and saying "No" to the adjuster's offer. No offense can be taken! In fact, it may even make the adjuster embarrassed at how low the offer was.

YOUR STRATEGY
"WALK AWAY" FROM THE NEGOTIATING TABLE
IF YOU DON'T LIKE THE OFFER.

Just because a claim is negotiable doesn't mean you have to negotiate. If you have all the documentation, there may be nothing to negotiate. When this is the situation, there is not much to lose by "walking away from the table." Remember, the adjuster wants to close your claim. To do that the adjuster knows an agreement must be reached. If you have negotiated all you are going to or if you are not willing to negotiate at all, walk away from the table and *mean it*! Have the will power to wait out the adjuster. Time is on your side. When negotiations resume, the offer may look surprisingly better.

YOUR STRATEGY
REQUEST A NEW ADJUSTER IF YOU CANNOT WORK
WITH THE ONE ASSIGNED TO YOUR CLAIM.

Many adjusters just love to haggle and the insurance claims business provides many opportunities for adjusters to hone their skills. Some negotiating is necessary on all claims. But, you shouldn't have to deal with any adjuster whose negotiating technics makes settling the claim like "pulling teeth."

As a policyholder, you are entitled to good faith and fair business dealings from the insurance company. Any adjuster who seems to be challenging you on the amount of your claim and who is not working with you toward settlement should be replaced. You will need to write a letter to the insurance company. Here is a sample letter:

Sample Letter to Remove The Adjuster From The Claim

XYZ Insurance Company
100 N. First Street
Los Angeles, California   99999

RE: Insured: Shirley Yorkiding   March 12, 199X
        Date of Loss: 01-17-199X
        Policy#: 1290-121212
        Claim#: 123-456-787

CERTIFIED MAIL, RETURN RECEIPT REQUESTED

Attention: Supervisor of Soe Obnoxious, Adjuster

Dear Sir,

(*Amend the following paragraphs to fit your situation*)
I advised my agent of my claim on 01-18-199X. On 02-08-9X, I received a telephone call from the adjuster, Mr. Obnoxious. He came to my home on 02-27-9X to inspect my damage. I have provided all the documents he requested. After attempting to discuss my estimates and personal property inventory, as well as my claim for additional living expense, it has become clear to me that Mr. Obnoxious is not meeting his obligations to me under the policy.

List all reasons here.   Examples could be:

- The adjuster was rude.

- The adjuster failed to properly measure all rooms or examine all damage.

- The adjuster was argumentative.

- The adjuster was unwilling to discuss my estimate with my contractor.

- The adjuster won't return telephone calls.
- The adjuster is trying to force me to use a different contractor.

I cannot work with anyone who treats me this way or is unwilling to discuss my claim in good faith. Please assign another adjuster to my claim and advise me as soon as possible.

Sincerely,

Shirley Yorkiding

CC: (your insurance agent)

CHAPTER 5

COLLECTING FOR THE DAMAGE TO YOUR HOME

If the initial rocking and rolling didn't devastate your home, the after shocks and weather conditions following the earthquake may. And then there are broken water pipes, power related problems, looting, vandalism and even fires! All the various types of repairs that may be necessary to your home are not covered in this chapter—there are just too many possibilities to mention. What is covered are the items of damage most often overlooked, coverages that often go unclaimed, and the common problems that are encountered while estimating damage to your home. You will inevitably run into one or more of these situations.

YOUR STRATEGY
BEWARE OF THE ADJUSTER'S "OFFICIAL" PRICE GUIDE.

Every adjuster has an "official" price guide to use when estimating the costs to repair your damage. A price guide is created after an insurance company reaches an agreement with one or more contractors who agree to work at these pre-determined prices (often the pricing is agreed to *before* the earthquake). The insurance company then types up the agreed prices, photocopies and staples together a couple hundred copies and—presto!—the "official" price guide.

Big deal? The insurance companies must think so—they try to hold all contractors and policyholders to it. Smaller insurance companies even copy the larger insurance companies' price guides (making the pricing look even *more* "official"). It is not uncommon by the fourth or fifth week after a disaster, for every insurance adjuster in town to be using the same "official" price guide.

Bottom line—the price guide isn't "official" at all. It is an attempt by insurance companies to simplify claims and control prices. So recognize that while a price guide is useful to insurance companies, the prices are not etched in stone, no matter what the adjuster tells you. The price guide is exactly that—a guide!

YOUR STRATEGY
RELY ON THE CONTRACTOR'S ESTIMATE
—NOT THE ADJUSTER'S ESTIMATE—
FOR CORRECT PRICING AND REPAIR PROCEDURES.

The adjuster *has* to write an estimate of your damage to document the claim file and get you paid—with or without a contractor being involved. Allowing the adjuster to estimate your claim and write you a check based on that estimate may seem like such a fast and easy way to get the claim handled. But that is exactly what the insurance company wants you to do—accept its pricing and repair procedures, without the input of a contractor, no questions asked.

As a rule, without the involvement of a contractor, the adjuster will settle the claim for *significantly* less than the amount a contractor will charge to do the proper repairs. And then *you* are left to the

51

task of negotiating with your contractor to lower his estimate or trying to squeeze more money out of the insurance company.

Although it takes a little more time, it is to your full benefit to have the adjuster reach an agreement with your contractor on the correct pricing and proper repairs *before* settling your claim. And what the insurance company will have as documentation to pay your claim is the adjuster's estimate that is tailored after your contractor's estimate.

YOUR STRATEGY
HAVE THE ADJUSTER FIGURE
CUSTOM REPAIR PRICES.

Most adjusters write estimates with computer programs using their "official" price guides. The adjuster eyeballs your damage and room size—then tries to make the prices for generic repair procedures and generic grades of material fit your situation.

Quality craftsmanship and custom work is always more expensive, so be sure to point out any damage to "custom" items that need repaired or replaced. Once the adjuster is made aware of custom features, the adjuster may have to find a creative way to come up with a price (because custom items and repair methods are not in the "price guide").

YOUR STRATEGY
AVOID BEING TRAPPED BY THE
"EARTH MOVEMENT EXCLUSION."

Earth movement means; settling, sinking, mud slide, bulging, expanding, erosion, etc. All policies have an earth movement exclusion, even when earthquake coverage is purchased. Adjusters like to use this exclusion if they can convince you that your damage is "old" damage and was caused by settling, sinking, expanding—in other words, EARTH MOVEMENT!

The adjuster will be looking at your damage for telltale signs that the damage is not new. If the cracks in your floors, patios, driveways, walls, or ceilings are "fresh," the edges will be clean and sharp. If the cracks are "old," they will have paint, dust or dirt accumulation in them. If the damage does not appear "fresh" (caused by the earthquake) the adjuster may want to deny your claim for that part of the damage and base the denial on the earth movement exclusion.

To avoid being trapped by this exclusion, you must show the adjuster the difference between new and old damage. You should be able to recognize and show the adjuster when an old crack has widened or worsened. Just because a crack was present before the earthquake does not mean you cannot claim *additional* damage to the original crack.

YOUR STRATEGY
HAVE YOUR CHIMNEY INSPECTED—BOTH INSIDE AND OUT.

Have the chimney inspected closely both inside and out to see if there is damage. Any cracks may pose a potential fire hazard to your home. Cracks are hard to spot, so have an expert carefully examine the chimney, firebox and flue. A cracked flue is not only unsafe but could justify payment for a replacement of the entire chimney.

If there are exterior cracks to your chimney, some insurance companies will have their engineer drop a video camera down the chimney to check for internal cracks. If none are seen on the amateur movie, the chimney is declared "safe" and the engineer may recommend paying only for cosmetic repairs. If this is your situation, you may want to get a second opinion—so hire your own expert!

YOUR STRATEGY
LOOK FOR DAMAGE TO YOUR FOUNDATION.

I cannot begin to tell you the number of adjusters who did not even check foundations when estimating damage to homes from the Northridge Earthquake in Los Angeles County in 1994. Many adjusters simply do not know what to look for, don't want to spend the extra time looking for foundation damage or feel uneasy about crawling under a house or building.

If you have a cracked foundation, you may be on your own to point out the damage so you can get paid. Here is a check list to help you find out if there is foundation damage:

✔**Walk around the perimeter of the house, garage or any masonry structures** to look for cracks. Start from the ground up. Often these are only hairline cracks and hard to see.

✔**Use a powerful flashlight** and examine all concrete under the house to see if there are cracks. Not all foundation cracks show up on the exterior. If you feel unsafe or uneasy about doing this yourself, have your contractor do the inspection.

✔**When you find a crack, mark it with a grease pencil** so you can easily point it out to the adjuster, contractor or engineer.

✔**If your house is on a concrete slab foundation, you need to feel through the carpet or floor covering** barefoot or on your hands and knees to check for uneven places or cracks in the concrete. Be very thorough—neither the adjuster nor a contractor will take the time to do this.

✔**If you have hardwood floors, get close to the floor** and look for uneven planks.

Once cracks are discovered, your contractor or engineer can best describe the method of repair. Do not leave this to the adjuster.

> **Note:** Some slab cracks cannot be felt or seen without pulling up the carpet or floor covering. Use a four foot or longer level to help detect these cracks.

YOUR STRATEGY
HAVE YOUR HEATING AND AIR CONDITIONING UNITS INSPECTED BY A QUALIFIED REPAIRER.

Heating and air conditioning units should be inspected by a qualified repair person. The efficiency may drop in these units due to damage, lowering their life expectancy.

Incidentally, these units usually are covered for damage caused by a power surge (power surges are common during and following a major earthquake). Since heating and central air conditioning units are considered part of the dwelling, you should get replacement cost coverage if they need to be replaced.

YOUR STRATEGY
OPEN AND CLOSE ALL YOUR WINDOWS.

Windows do not have to have broken glass to be damaged. An earthquake can easily damage a window frame. If your window opening is cracked or no longer square, it will affect how easily the window goes up and down. Open and close each window to check for difficulty in sliding. If you have this problem, you may be entitled to a new window unit.

YOUR STRATEGY
REQUEST TO REPLACE—NOT TO PATCH—CRACKED PLASTER OR DRYWALL.

It is common for an adjuster to estimate a patch here and a patch there to repair the damaged drywall and plaster, instead of just replacing it or completely skim coating the plastered wall. Unless the damage is *very* minimal, request the entire wall be replaced.

YOUR STRATEGY
FOLLOW THE "CLEAR LINE OF VISION" PRINCIPLE FOR ALL REPAIRS TO YOUR HOME.

When the damage to your home requires replacement of items and the replaced items do not match the existing material, the insurance company should replace all items in the "clear line of vision" to maintain a uniform appearance.

For example, you have damage to one wall in a room. You can't just paint over the damaged area and expect it to match the rest of the wall or room. You will need to paint all the walls that match the damaged wall until the change in color is out of your "clear line of vision."

Here's another example: you have a small area of damage to the wallpaper in your living room. The wallpaper is the same pattern from the living room, down the hall and into the kitchen. If you can stand in your living room and see the hall, and you can stand in your hall and see the kitchen, that is a "clear line of vision." You should request replacement of the wallpaper (unless you can get an *identical* match) in the living room, down the hall and throughout the kitchen. The "clear line of vision" principle should always be considered for the interior and exterior of your home when any of the following items are damaged:

- **ALL FLOOR COVERINGS:** Carpet, Vinyl, Wood, Tile, etc.

- **PAINT:** Interior and exterior.

- **EXTERIOR SIDING**

- **WALLPAPER**

- **PANELING**

- **TILE OR LAMINATE COUNTER TOPS**

- **BATH OR SHOWER TILE**

- **CABINETS**

- **BATHROOM FIXTURES:** Toilet, Bath, Sink etc.

YOUR STRATEGY
REQUEST NEW CARPETING WHEN YOUR CARPET GETS GLASS IN IT OR HAS WATER DAMAGE.

Other than by total destruction, carpeting can be damaged several ways. For example:

- **BROKEN GLASS.** You may be unable to get all the glass slivers out of the fibers of the carpet.

- **RAIN, AQUARIUM OR POOL WATER.** Water contains micro-organisms that may create a smell in the carpet and padding. Shampoo and disinfectant treatments cannot remove them all. Consider replacing all carpet that gets wet from these sources.

Once it is determined you need to replace *any* area of the carpet—no matter how small the area is—the "clear line of vision" principle should apply. As long as the carpet is contiguous, (the same carpet throughout your home) all of your carpet should be replaced.

Prices for removal of old carpet and installation of new carpet vary quite a bit as you would expect. Most adjuster price guides do not adequately cover the different types of carpet and most adjusters are not very good at identifying grades of carpet. So, do not accept a settlement on carpeting without getting an estimate to replace your grade of carpet and pad.

Items Frequently Overlooked In The Estimating Process

✔**Your labor** for any time spent to clean up, remove debris, or make temporary repairs. (Usually an hourly rate equivalent to the charge by a person specializing in that trade.)

✔**Washing and prepping** walls and ceilings before painting. (Usually a price per square foot; exterior and interior.)

✔**Roofs.** Often roofs are inadequately inspected or completely overlooked. Most adjusters are accustomed to looking at wind and hail damaged roofs and do not know what to look for after an earthquake. Tile or concrete roofs are particularly vulnerable to earthquake damage.

✔**Masking** off before painting. (Usually a price per linear foot.)

✔**Removing, replacing or resetting fixtures.** Lighting, fan vents, towel racks, shelving, etc., should be removed for access to do repairs or paint. (Usually a price per fixture.)

✔**Removing and replacing furniture** to do repairs or paint. (Usually a price per room depending on the number and size of items.)

✔**Removing and replacing ceiling and floor moldings** to repair and paint.

✔**Trash and debris removal** for the original cleanup, waste, trash, and debris from the repair process. (Usually a *highly* negotiable dollar amount, often calculated as a percentage of the total estimate of damage. Five percent is common.)

✔**Clean up and washing** of anything. (Usually a price per item or per room.)

✔**Fees and permits.** (Usually fees assessed by local governmental agencies.)

✔**Sandblasting** off old paint and stucco before repainting. (Usually a price per square foot)

✔**Color coating** exterior stucco walls after sandblasting and repairing the damage. (Usually a price per square foot.)

✔**Shampooing carpets** may be necessary if you have any repairs being done inside your home even if your carpet was not damaged from the earthquake. (Repair people are going to be tramping all over your carpets!) Shampooing carpets generally should *not* be considered a method of repair if the carpets are damaged by the earthquake. (Usually a price per square foot.)

✔**Including trim work** in a paint job.

✔**Including all cracks** in the estimate. Many are missed around windows hidden by drapes and window coverings. (Usually involves painting the room and wall repair.)

✔**Nicks or gouges in counter tops** may not be repairable (even if they are small). Most counter tops have to be completely replaced. If there is a sink or built in appliance involved in replacing the counter top, there also may be plumbing and electrical (removing and resetting) charges to claim. (Usually a price by the job.)

✔**Including enough materials to account for waste** in roofing, vinyl flooring, carpeting, wallpaper, etc. (Waste can increase an estimate up to 20% depending on the type of repairs!)

✔**Including insulation** in the attic, walls, or floors—if it gets wet. Many adjusters may try to tell you, "Once the insulation dries out it will be fine." Not always true! R-value may be lost and it may begin to smell badly from micro-organisms left after the water dries. Request new insulation and have your contractor verify the need to replace it. (Usually a price per square foot.)

YOUR STRATEGY
COMPARE YOUR ROOM DIMENSIONS TO THOSE LISTED ON THE ADJUSTER'S ESTIMATE.

Adjusters may not accurately measure and record all the damaged rooms, so take your own room measurements and check them against the adjuster's estimate. If your room dimensions (or damages) are different from those listed on the adjuster's estimate, request the damage be reinspected!

YOUR STRATEGY
HAVE THE ADJUSTER EXPLAIN—IN DETAIL—THE ENTIRE ESTIMATE TO YOU, ITEM BY ITEM.

To make sure you have been paid for everything you are owed, you must understand what the adjuster included in the estimate. Have the adjuster explain it to you—each line, item by item. If you don't understand something, have the adjuster go over it with you until you do.

Mobile Home Specific

There are many ways a mobile home may be damaged without being an obvious total loss. This damage, when properly estimated, can result in what the insurance companies call a "constructive total loss." This means the cost to repair the mobile home exceeds its value.

It is very important to obtain the services of a contractor who specializes in mobile home repair to help you in assessing any damage. Mobile homes are estimated differently from "on site" built homes. There are many unique features within mobile homes that are not found in other homes. Besides the items previously listed in this chapter, here are some "mobile home specific" items that you and your contractor should check:

✔**The roof.** Most metal roofs will need to be, at the very least, re-membraned and sealed if they sustained any amount of movement or vibration.

✔**The marriage wall.** If you have a double wide, the wall that combines the two units often separates (even a slight separation can lead to future water damage). A quick way to check for separation is by examining the floor and carpet where the two walls meet to see if the floor is uneven or if there is a gap.

✔**The steel "I" frame.** Most mobile homes are built on steel "I" frames. If your home came off its blocks, it is likely there was frame damage. Sometimes the twisting of the frame can easily be seen with a naked eye. Other times the home must be blocked and reset before frame damage can be determined. An uneven floor is one indicator of frame damage.

Where and how the frame is damaged will decide whether the mobile home is repairable. This is very serious damage and is often overlooked by adjusters. If you have this type of damage, you may have a "constructive total loss" which means the cost to repair it exceeds its value.

> **Note:** If it is determined that your mobile home is a total loss, your mobile home will be considered salvage. If you are interested in buying back your mobile home, read about salvage in the chapter, "Collecting For The Damage To Your Personal Property."

✔**The blocking and leveling system.** Damage will be obvious if the mobile home came completely off its blocks or foundation, but slight shifts may *not* be so obvious. The mobile home should be level. You can measure this yourself with a four foot level.

✔**The plumbing (including hot water heater), heating and cooling units, duct work and the electrical supply.** Have your contractor supply names or find your own qualified repairer to inspect these systems. Remember, everything has been vibrated and shaken around. Damage is likely.

✔**The Insulation.** All walls, sides, ceiling, and underbelly have insulation. When it gets wet from broken pipes or roof leaks, it can compress, losing much of its ability to insulate. The wet insulation can harbor micro-organisms. A favorite tactic of insurance companies is to have the adjuster tell you to let the insulation dry out and it will be okay. Of course the company isn't concerned if you spend more for heating and cooling your home now that the R-value of the insulation has dropped! Insist on replacing all wet insulation and have the contractor verify the need.

✔**The Siding.** Check closely where the siding panels are attached to the mobile home. Nails, rivets, or screws regularly loosen or pop out during an earthquake. Remember the "clear line of vision principle" and insist on replacement of panels with like kind, quality, and texture.

✔**The Windows.** If your home is not level, your windows won't be square. Open and close all windows to check for damage to frames.

CHAPTER **6**

IS YOUR HOME UNLIVABLE?

There are many ways your home can be damaged during and following an earthquake. Once you have "DIRECT" DAMAGE TO YOUR PROPERTY and your home is unlivable, you may be entitled to payment for expenses to live elsewhere. This coverage is called "**Additional Living Expense**." You also may be entitled to this coverage if your home becomes unlivable while it is being repaired—even if your home is livable after the earthquake.

> **Note:** "Direct" means *specifically* to your home. For example, if your power is out, to qualify for Additional Living Expense coverage, the power line or transformer that cuts off your power must be ON YOUR PROPERTY. If you have no water, it must be due to damage of the water lines ON YOUR PROPERTY.

YOUR STRATEGY
YOU MUST DETERMINE WHETHER YOUR HOME IS UNLIVABLE.

Sometimes it is obvious your home is unlivable (like if it is demolished). Other times, it may not be so obvious. It is a judgment call *you* make. While the insurance company can always challenge your judgment, it probably won't if you have a good reason. Here are a few possible reasons:

REASONS A HOME MAY BE UNLIVABLE

- **DIRECT DAMAGE TO YOUR HOME MAKING IT UNINHABITABLE.**

- **SAFETY**—Believing your home is structurally unsafe.

- **DANGEROUS CONDITIONS TO YOUR HEALTH** which make living in your house intolerable. For example: gas leaks, toxic or obnoxious fumes, pregnancy risks, asthma attacks, allergies to exposed materials (such as allergic reactions to insulation,) unsafe living conditions for infants, small children and elderly, etc. Obtain a note from your physician *if* your adjuster requests documentation.

- **IF THE POLICE, NATIONAL GUARD, OR CITY INSPECTORS PROHIBIT ACCESS TO YOUR PROPERTY**. Even if there is no damage to your property, you may be able to collect Additional Living Expense coverage for up to two weeks.

- **YOUR HOME IS WITHOUT WATER**—You can't exactly bathe in jugs of drinking water from the grocery store.

- **YOUR HOME IS WITHOUT POWER**—Wanting air conditioning and hot showers is not unreasonable. For more information, see the power outage topic in the chapter "Collecting For The Damage To Your Personal Property."

Remember, if you have no power or water and that is the *only* reason your home is unlivable, the damage to the broken water pipe or the power line must be on *your* property to qualify for Additional Living Expense coverage.

YOUR STRATEGY
UNDERSTAND THE RULES OF "ADDITIONAL LIVING EXPENSE" COVERAGE TO MAXIMIZE YOUR PAYMENT.

Additional Living Expense coverage is often overlooked and misunderstood. The amounts you can claim are those costs that are "additional" to your normal living costs. The term "additional" means the *increase* in cost of living beyond your normal cost of living. Here is a list of common additional living expenses and how they are typically calculated:

COMMON ADDITIONAL LIVING EXPENSES

- **RENT OR HOTEL**

- **ADDITIONAL UTILITIES**

- **RESTAURANT OR FOOD PREPARATION CHARGES**

- **ANY ADDITIONAL DRIVING YOU DO** to maintain your standard of living. A charge for mileage can be anywhere from $.25 to $.45 per mile.

- **ADDITIONAL COSTS OF DRY CLEANING AND LAUNDERING CLOTHING**

- **ADDITIONAL COSTS FOR PRIVATE TRANSPORTATION** for children to and from school or other events.

- **ADDITIONAL TELEPHONE EXPENSES**

- **MOVING PROPERTY TO A NEW LOCATION** for use or storage.

- **GENERATOR RENTAL**

- **PET BOARDING** (Monkeys, chickens, goats, pigs or any animal you call a pet.)

- TELEPHONE AND UTILITY HOOK UP FEES

- RENTAL DEPOSITS

- ANYTHING ELSE REASONABLE AND NECESSARY TO MAINTAIN YOUR STANDARD OF LIVING

ADDITIONAL LIVING EXPENSE CALCULATION

COST OF LIVING BEFORE		NEW COST OF LIVING
Mortgage:	$2,500.00	Rent/Hotel: $95.00 x 30 days=$2,850.00 ($2500.00 mortgage payment stays constant)

NET ADDITIONAL EXPENSE: **$2,850.00**

Utilities:	$375.00	Utilities while unoccupied: $175.00

NET ADDITIONAL EXPENSE: **$<200.00>**   (This is a reduction)

Food:	$600.00	Cost of eating out: $900.00

NET ADDITIONAL EXPENSE: **$300.00**   (The amount above what you normally spend)

Pet Boarding: (for the Goat)	$00.00	Pet Boarding: $10.00 x 30 days=$300.00

NET ADDITIONAL EXPENSE: **$300.00**

MONTHLY ADDITIONAL LIVING EXPENSE TOTAL: $3,250.00

This basic illustration only scratches the surface of the types of additional costs you may have. Save every receipt. Anything that is necessary to continue your normal standard of living after the earthquake and is beyond what you normally spend, may be reimbursed under Additional Living Expense coverage.

YOUR STRATEGY
REQUEST AN "ADVANCE PAYMENT" FOR PROJECTED ADDITIONAL LIVING EXPENSE COSTS.

It is easy to forget or overlook expenses you have incurred after you have *spent* the money. So request an advance payment for additional living expense—up front. If you have not been called by the adjuster yet, ask your agent for it. You also can make your request directly to the insurance company. An easy to use, fill-in the-blank form to request an advance payment for Additional Living Expense coverage, is included in the **CLAIM SIMPLI-FILER**. (To order, see the appendix.)

Unless it is obvious you must be out of your home, some adjusters will avoid mentioning Additional Living Expense coverage. The adjuster knows that if you do not ask for it, it probably won't have to be calculated or paid.

When you do ask for an advance for additional living expense, don't accept "turn in your receipts when you incur them" as your answer. This may be an effort by the adjuster to avoid paying you up front for this expense. While some insurance companies are willing to pay the expense in advance, some adjusters avoid the extra paper work involved with this part of the claim. If the adjuster insists there is no additional living expense advance, call the adjuster's immediate supervisor and request an advance.

YOUR STRATEGY
GET WRITTEN DOCUMENTATION TO MAXIMIZE ADDITIONAL LIVING EXPENSE "ADVANCE PAYMENTS."

Since written documentation is more persuasive, get an estimate for moving and storage of your personal property. Get a quotation for the cost to rent a comparable home for the period your home will be under repair (cut out a newspaper classified ad). Get a quotation for pet boarding, write down the additional miles you are driving, etc. The more you have in writing, the more willing the insurance company will be to give you an advance payment.

YOUR STRATEGY
CHOOSE THE MORE EXPENSIVE HOUSING IF COMPARABLE HOUSING IS NOT AVAILABLE.

Get a castle for a castle when you have to move out of your home. If comparable housing is not available, move up to the higher priced accommodations. You should not have to settle for a decrease in standard of living. You are entitled to at least the same quality of living that your previously undamaged home provided and all the incidental charges involved in getting you there!

YOUR STRATEGY
IF YOUR HOME BECOMES UNLIVABLE—DURING REPAIRS—REQUEST A PAYMENT UNDER ADDITIONAL LIVING EXPENSE COVERAGE.

I would bet that Additional Living Expense coverage for the period of time your home is under repair is overlooked by the adjuster in nine out of every ten claims. *You* won't overlook it! If you know that your home will be partially or totally unlivable during the repairs, request payment—up front—for your projected expenses.

The best time to request Additional Living Expense coverage is *before* the repair process begins. If the repairs are underway or complete, the only amount you can be reimbursed is the actual funds you have paid out. Keep documentation and receipts!

YOUR STRATEGY
SIGN A PROMISSORY NOTE WHEN STAYING WITH FRIENDS OR RELATIVES.

Friends or relatives may be willing to house you and your family after a disaster.   If you meet the requirements and can get Additional Living Expense coverage, they shouldn't have to house you for free. You should decide a reasonable amount per night for housing and sign a simple promissory note. This qualifies as having incurred the expense, though you may not have exchanged funds. Use comparable hotel expense as a guide.

Here is a sample promissory note:

*Promissory Note For Lodging Expenses

I, the undersigned promise to pay to:

_____

the total amount of $ _____. This amount is for

lodging for the time period of _____ to_____
                              (date beginning)   (date ending)

at the rate of $_____ per _____while my
                             (day, week or month)

home was unlivable.

_____

Signature   Date

*(This obligates you to a debt)

CHAPTER 7

COLLECTING FOR THE DAMAGE TO YOUR "OTHER STRUCTURES"

What are "Other Structures?"

Other structures or "appurtenant private structures" (the term sometimes used in the insurance policies) are those structures around your home. They include: **fences, swimming pools, decks, driveways, sidewalks,** and **unattached garages, barns** or **sheds** etc. Generally, buildings are insured at replacement cost and items other than buildings are insured at actual cash value (subject to depreciation).

The amount of coverage you have for "other structures" should be listed on the **DECLARATIONS PAGE** of your policy. It is usually 10% of the amount of coverage you have on your home. (The 10% is in *addition* to the amount of coverage you have on your home.)

The structures most often damaged from an earthquake are outbuildings, fences, sidewalks, patios, driveways, and pools—so don't forget to check to see if these items are damaged. The information that follows in this chapter should help you when inspecting your property so you can point out the damage to the adjuster and to your contractor. It also will help you present your claim for "other structures" coverage.

Driveways, Garage Floors, Sidewalks, Retaining Walls, and Patios

Driveways, garage floors, sidewalks, retaining walls, and patios are typically concrete (masonry) or asphalt. All may show signs of earthquake damage and should be closely inspected.

YOUR STRATEGY
GET PAID FOR YOUR OLD CRACKS WHEN THEY ARE MADE WORSE BY THE EARTHQUAKE.

Let's say you had one or two cracks in your driveway before the earthquake. After the earthquake you closely examine your driveway and discover the old cracks are worse. When previous cracks worsen, you can make a claim to have the cracks repaired even though the original cracks were old.

YOUR STRATEGY
DO NOT ACCEPT CONCRETE PATCH JOBS.

Many insurance companies only want to pay you to patch the concrete or fill the cracks and leave it at that. Yet, that is not the correct repair and you are entitled to be paid to have the correct repairs done. The "correct repair" means *replacing* the concrete—so ask for it! Driveways, sidewalks, retaining walls and patios are subject to depreciation, so don't forget to negotiate the depreciation amounts. For more information see the chapter, "Replacement Cost Coverage And Depreciation."

Unattached Garages, Barns and Storage Sheds

Since unattached garages, barns or storage sheds are buildings, they are usually NOT SUBJECT TO DEPRECIATION under a replacement cost policy. This means you should get the full cost to replace or repair these buildings if you have replacement cost coverage on your home.

YOUR STRATEGY
APPROACH THE REPAIRS TO YOUR OUTBUILDINGS THE SAME AS YOU DO YOUR HOME.

Use the same strategies and follow the same procedures to estimate the damage to your unattached garages, barns and storage sheds as you do your home. Have your contractor break down the repair charges per building and itemize the repair procedures. Try to be prepared with the contractor's estimate *before* the adjuster inspects the damage.

Total losses to unattached structures are common in a major earthquake. If you have many outbuildings, your damages may quickly exceed your limit of coverage.

> **Note:** The personal items stored within the outbuildings are considered personal property. See the chapter, "Collecting For The Damage To Your Personal Property," to file a claim for the damage to contents of your outbuildings.

YOUR STRATEGY
CHECK YOUR GARAGE DOOR JAMB.

Just because your unattached garage is still standing, doesn't mean it is not damaged. It is common for an earthquake to cause a garage to shift on its foundation, leaving the structure itself to remain intact. If the earthquake causes the garage to move, even slightly, at its foundation, the garage is damaged.

Check the garage door jamb. Movement of the structure on its foundation is most noticeable at the jamb or frame of the garage where the door meets the foundation. Look for any signs of movement to a painted wall such as newly exposed unpainted areas (where obviously the wall had to have shifted to expose the unpainted area), difficulty opening the garage door, new cracks in the foundation, etc. Put a level to the walls to see if the walls are still plumb. Unless you point out this type of damage to the contractor or adjuster, the damage could be overlooked.

Swimming Pools

If you own a pool, get a qualified pool service to thoroughly check everything from your filtering system to the coping. Swimming pools can be damaged many ways during and following an earthquake and pool damage is often overlooked by owners, adjusters and contractors alike.

COMMON DAMAGE TO POOLS

- **CRACKS AROUND THE DRAIN.**

- **CRACKS IN THE POOL FLOOR.**

- **CRACKED OR LOOSENED COPING.**

- **CRACKED OR LOOSENED TILES.**

- **CLOGGED OR INOPERABLE FILTERING SYSTEMS.**

- **BROKEN OR LOOSE PLUMBING.**

- **STAINING FROM FOREIGN DEBRIS** floating or lying in the bottom.

If your pool construction is of a certain type of material, make sure the estimate for replacement is of equal value. You are entitled to the same quality of materials you had. Even if the material is no longer available, the insurance company owes you for what it would take to replace it with "like kind and quality."

YOUR STRATEGY
HAVE THE INSURANCE COMPANY CHANGE YOUR POOL WATER AND CHEMICALS.

Well, the insurance company won't actually do the changing, but it probably will pay you to have it done! Depending on the type of damage to your pool, water replacement, acid washing of the pool and cleaning the filtering system may be necessary and is usually a covered expense. Don't forget—if you spend any time working on your pool, make a claim for your labor.

Refilling the pool and balancing the water pH also can be claimed as an expense. What the municipal water company charges you per gallon of water multiplied by the number of gallons your pool holds is the most accurate way to figure the cost to refill the pool. Provide receipts for the cost of the chemicals to balance the water.

Wood Fences and Block Walls

Wood fences and block walls are "other structures." They are SUBJECT TO DEPRECIATION, even if replacement cost coverage applies to your buildings. Block walls last a long time, so very little depreciation should be taken. On the other hand, wood fences do not last as long and can be assessed *significant* depreciation.

YOUR STRATEGY
DON'T REPLACE THE ENTIRE WOOD FENCE UNLESS IT IS ABSOLUTELY NECESSARY.

If you keep some part of the old fence and do not replace the fence completely, the fence repair is *not* subject to depreciation—A COMPLETE REPLACEMENT IS! By using a post or two or some pickets from your old fence, the fence won't have to be "completely" replaced—it will just need a very "extensive repair!" Don't let the adjuster pay to replace your fence completely *unless* you can live with the amount of depreciation that will be assessed.

Common Walls and Fences

Insurance adjusters typically assume that any wall or fence between you and your neighbor is jointly owned. But who really owns the walls or fences that are located between you and your neighbor? Find out. The wall or fence may be owned jointly (in "common") or, *you* may be the sole owner. If there is evidence your neighbor owns half, then you are only entitled to collect half of the repair or replacement. But—if the fence is *solely* on your property and there is no evidence to the contrary, then you probably own it all. The adjuster should not just guess that you only own half just because the wall *looks* like it is on the property line!

If you are the sole owner, you are entitled to full payment for all repairs to your fence or wall. If it becomes an issue, send a certified letter to support your claim. Here is a sample letter:

Sample Letter To Support Your Claim For Full Payment For Your Fence Or Block Wall

XYZ Insurance Company
100 N. First Street
Los Angeles, CA 90000

RE: Insured: Itsa Mifence   February 11, 199X
       Date of Loss: 01-17-199X
       Policy#: 1290-121212
       Claim#: 123-456-788

Attention: Betshe Takeshaph, Adjuster

Dear Ms. Takeshaph,

I am the sole owner of the (*fence/block wall*) situated on the (*east west, north, south side, or surrounding*) my property. I have discussed this matter with my neighbor and she is in agreement. If you have evidence to the contrary please provide it to me immediately. Otherwise, I expect payment in full for the damage to the above property.

Sincerely,

Itsa Mifence

CHAPTER 8

COLLECTING FOR THE DAMAGE TO YOUR PERSONAL PROPERTY

Personal property encompasses a wide range of things—glassware, computers, cooking oil, buttons, lumber, spices, books, lawn mowers, Christmas decorations, inoperable vehicles (if they're up on blocks), panty hose, pork chops and paintings. It is everything that is *not* a building or other structure.

YOUR STRATEGY
MAKE A LIST—AND CHECK IT TWICE.

Start by making a list of *everything* that is damaged—even if it has no personal value to you. Simple-to-use personal property inventory sheets are included in the **CLAIM SIMPLI-FILER** (to order, see the appendix) or you can use the forms provided by the adjuster. Every damaged item should be claimed—even if the damage is minor. For each item, list the following:

- **DESCRIPTION OF THE PROPERTY.**
  Brand, make, model, serial number etc.

- **ANY SPECIAL FEATURES THE ITEM HAD.**
  Personalized items, upgrades, custom made items etc.

- **THE DATE PURCHASED OR ACQUIRED.**
  If you can remember!

- **THE PRESENT COST—PLUS <u>TAX AND DELIVERY</u>.**
  Cost to replace this item with LIKE KIND, and QUALITY.

YOUR STRATEGY
USE A MAGNIFYING GLASS WHEN VIEWING YOUR PHOTOGRAPHS.

You took photographs of your damage, right? Now you can use those photographs to recall those items you may have forgotten. Use a magnifying glass, when viewing your photographs, to help you identify all your contents. The magnifying glass works particularly well when you have many items of personal property visible in the picture.

If you have no photographs or if your property is gone for whatever reason, **"THE TOTAL RECALL PROPERTY INVENTORY LIST"** is very helpful and is included in the **CLAIMS SIMPLI-FILER**. It is an extensive list, alphabetized *and* by room, of typical items of personal property and will help jog your memory.

YOUR STRATEGY
USE CATALOGUES TO PROVIDE YOU WITH THE CURRENT REPLACEMENT COST OF YOUR PERSONAL PROPERTY.

There is no reason to run all over town trying to find the replacement cost of your damaged personal property—just use catalogues. There are mail order catalogues which contain almost every type of personal property you can imagine. And you don't need to order from the catalogue unless you want to.

YOUR STRATEGY
GET WRITTEN ESTIMATES TO REPLACE ITEMS OF UNKNOWN VALUE OR VALUES HIGHER THAN $250.00.

Getting written estimates to replace higher value items may seem like a hassle, but written estimates are powerful! Estimates actually *eliminate* many hassles—an *expert* puts in writing the value of your property. Use retail stores, TV and appliance technicians, antique appraisers or anyone else qualified to determine the present retail value of your specific property.

YOUR STRATEGY
IF YOU CANNOT GET A WRITTEN ESTIMATE ON THE PRICE OF YOUR PERSONAL PROPERTY, DON'T BE AFRAID TO GUESS AT THE REPLACEMENT VALUE.

The preferred method of documenting your damage is to get written quotations for replacement of those items of unknown value and values over $250.00. There will be times, however, when no one will know what an item is worth (that ceramic donkey from Aunt Carole—what's it worth???).

"Guesstimate" if you are not certain. This is what the adjuster probably will do. The important point here is for *you* to put prices on every item—don't let the adjuster do the "guesstimating" on the value of *your* property!

YOUR STRATEGY
ALWAYS INCLUDE SALES TAX AND DELIVERY CHARGES.

Sales tax and delivery charges are covered expenses and are often overlooked in settlements. When getting quotations to replace personal property, always include the estimate for state and local sales tax as well as delivery charges to your home.

YOUR STRATEGY
THE PRICE YOU PAID FOR YOUR PROPERTY HAS NO BEARING ON THE AMOUNT YOU CAN CLAIM. (YOUR CLAIM IS *NOT* A GARAGE SALE!)

When asked to give the current replacement cost, I cannot tell you the number of times I have seen people write down their actual purchase price (from 1952), or what they *feel* an item is worth if they sold it at a yard or garage sale. You should list the price of each item of personal property at its PRESENT DAY COST TO REPLACE FROM A RETAIL STORE OR CATALOGUE. For example:

> *You bought a compressor used for $300.00.*

> *The garage roof fell on it in the earthquake and now it doesn't work.*

> *Today's new cost of the compressor is $498.00 plus $84.86 sales tax and delivery.*

You should list $582.86 as the current replacement cost.

YOUR STRATEGY
INSIST ON THE EXACT PRODUCT—MAKE, MODEL AND SPECIAL FEATURES—IF THE INSURANCE COMPANY USES A "BUYER'S SERVICE" PROGRAM.

Many insurance companies have arranged to purchase products from suppliers at prices less than full retail. This is a way the company saves money. If your company is using a "buyer's service" program, you will be offered what it costs the *insurance company* to replace your property—and no more.

Now if the question hasn't already entered your mind, what if you just bought the compressor for $582.86 instead of used for $300.00, as in the example? Your choices will be: have the compressor replaced or accept the amount it will cost the *insurance company* to replace it through the "buyer's service"—but not the $582.86.

The insurance company buyer's service program is not too bad as long as you get "apples for apples." By insisting on an exact replacement instead of a "similar" product you may be able to receive a payment closer to the actual retail replacement cost of your property. If the adjuster can match the make, model and special features of your item, have the company deliver it to you—if you *want* it replaced. If you do not want it replaced, or want *something else* in its place, you have no other choice than to accept the dollar amount for which the insurance company can replace the item.

YOUR STRATEGY
DO NOT ACCEPT AN "APPEARANCE ALLOWANCE."

An "appearance allowance" is a term that means you are paid an "allowance" for cosmetic damage (scratches, dents, nicks, tears, etc.) instead of the cost to properly repair or replace the item. Do not accept it! You are owed payment for the cost to *properly* repair or replace the damaged item—not an "allowance" to overlook it. Often, when properly estimated, the cost to repair the damage exceeds the cost to replace the item. So don't just live with damaged property and a few extra dollars to "put up with the new scars"—obtain estimates to properly repair or replace the item!

YOUR STRATEGY
IF THE ADJUSTER DEMANDS THAT YOU REPAIR YOUR PERSONAL PROPERTY, IT HAD BETTER BE TO YOUR SATISFACTION!

The adjuster may *insist* that you have your personal property repaired, refinished or cleaned as an initial attempt to settle your claim. If the adjuster demands that your property be repaired, remember, it must be done to *your* satisfaction!

Here is what you do:

- First, have the adjuster provide the name of the repairer.

- Then, require that the adjuster put in writing that the property will be replaced if the repairs are not done to your full satisfaction.

A sample letter, requesting this commitment follows:

Sample Request For Guaranteeing Replacement In The Event The Repairs Are Unsatisfactory

Insured:_____

Date of Loss: _____

Policy # _____

Claim # _____

I, _____representing

    (the adjuster)

_____Insurance Company

    (the Insurance Company name)

After having inspected the following described property:

_____

_____

at the home of,_____ on,_____,

    (Insured's name)   (date inspected)

determine that the above described property can be repaired. The

repairer who can perform the repairs is,_____

    (repair person)

If the repairs in an amount not to exceed $_____, fail

to meet this Insured's satisfaction, full replacement of the described

property will be paid by the above named Insurance Company.

Signed_____ Date_____

    (the adjuster)

YOUR STRATEGY
PROVIDE PROOF YOU OWNED THE DAMAGED ITEMS—*IF ASKED.*

You are required to show your damaged property. If—for whatever reason—your property is not available for inspection, you *may* be asked by the adjuster to prove you owned the property. Here are some ways to prove ownership:

> **BEST**—Provide a receipt, credit card sales slip or cancelled check for the purchase of the item.
>
> **BETTER**—Provide photos, owners manuals, or original packaging material of the items.

If you do not have any of the above, have a simple statement signed by someone who can, from personal knowledge, confirm that you owned the property.

> **GOOD ENOUGH**—Provide a statement signed by someone who knew you owned the item.

Here is a sample statement:

Sample Statement to Provide "Proof of Ownership" for Personal Property

Insured:_____

Date of Loss: _____

Policy # _____

Claim # _____

To whom it may concern:

I, _____observed the following

described property:

_____

_____

_____

_____

at the home of,   on,

_____   _____
(Insured's name)   (date last seen)

_____
(street address)

_____
(city, state & zip)

        Signed_____(observer)

        Date_____

        Telephone #_____

Items Often Incorrectly Claimed Or Overlooked When Listing Damage To Personal Property

✔**Wall hangings and pictures** including all types of artwork. In most policies, there is *no dollar limitation* for coverage to artwork, paintings or pictures (except the normal policy limitation on personal property). I routinely handle claims for people who do not make a serious effort to establish the value of their artwork. Call two or three art dealers to get estimates for replacement, at *today's* prices. It could be well worth the extra effort.

✔**Electronic components and TV's.** Unless the items are stolen by looters or are crushed by impact, when you make a claim for electronics, you must document the *cause* of the damage. Have a technician look at the item and write a short opinion about the cause of damage. The technician also can establish the cost of replacement and whether the item can be repaired. Insurance companies will usually pay for the fee charged for this service if the damage is caused by the earthquake.

✔**Furniture.** Short of total destruction, furniture can become scratched, nicked, torn, or stained. If your furniture is damaged in any way, start with the assumption that the furniture will be replaced. Get written prices for replacement of the furniture. Provide copies of the estimates to the adjuster.

✔**Fine china, stem ware, crystal, glassware and porcelain** cannot be repaired. One chip and they are history. Although you cannot make a claim for sentimental value, it is very important for you to find the prices of the items of the same quality as those that were broken. Whenever possible, get written estimates for replacing these items.

✔**Antiques or collectibles** are common in most homes. Some items that have been in your family for what seems like forever can possibly be valuable antiques or collectibles. The key is to get written appraisals for the cost to replace any item that *looks* antique!

Try to obtain appraisals from at least two antique dealers. They are usually *more* than willing to give you a quotation—for a fee. The insurance company may pay the fee. But even if it doesn't, $65.00 or so to appraise an old piano is worth it to find out that the piano was worth $12,500.00!

✔**Kitchen and laundry appliances** are damaged many ways other than just being crushed by a falling ceiling. The knobs and handles get broken. Porcelain gets gouged. They just stop working.

If you get pressured from the adjuster to settle for cosmetic repairs, ("appearance allowance" for touch ups to porcelain, etc.) use the "Sample Request For Guaranteeing Replacement In The Event Repairs Are Unsatisfactory" letter discussed earlier in the chapter.

If you suspect the earthquake caused a malfunction, the adjuster probably will want a repairer's written opinion to confirm the cause of damage. Like air conditioners and other electronic items, these appliances *are* subject to electrical damage. (See the power outage section of this chapter.)

✔**Jewelry, silverware, guns and furs.** Even adjusters I would give an A+ for thoroughness will miss this one! In the homeowners policy there are special limits for jewelry, silverware, guns and furs, but *the limits apply only to theft*—not to an earthquake! There is coverage up to policy limits for these items. So, follow the same plan for full recovery—appraisals and estimates for replacement at today's prices. If an exact item is not available, to insure an identical replacement, get a price to have the item(s) recreated by a gold or silversmith.

✔**Drapes, curtains, and blinds** require removal, cleaning and reinstallation in every room where painting, plastering or drywall repairs are to be done. These expenses can add up fast and are frequently missed.

YOUR STRATEGY
IF YOU "BUY BACK" YOUR SALVAGE, NEGOTIATE THE PRICE!

To understand what salvage is on personal property claims, think for a moment about an automobile claim. If the insurance company paid you for a total loss to your car, the insurance company would own the wrecked car. The company can keep the car (salvage) or sell the car (to you or anyone else).

Salvage of your personal property works the same way. The stereo, TV, couch, artwork, computer or any item you were paid to replace now belongs to the company. The company can keep the salvage, or sell it.

To become salvage, the item(s) must have some value left. Scratches on a table, for example, are ugly but will not make the table worthless. So if you are paid to replace the table, the insurance company owns the table as "salvage."

Here is where you come in—*you* are the preferred buyer of your salvage! It is the easiest way for the adjuster to "get rid of" your damaged but usable property. The adjuster simply agrees on a value with you, and subtracts that amount from your settlement check.

So if the subject of salvage is brought up by the adjuster—and you want to keep the item(s)—just remember, the adjuster does not want the hassle of selling your salvage to someone else, and should be eager to sell it to you at a price you just can't refuse.   So, ALWAYS NEGOTIATE salvage values!

> **Note:** And now a few words about the rotten apple.
> Always get a receipt from the adjuster if the adjuster
> *takes* your property for salvage.   A few adjusters take
> salvage and resell it for a *personal* profit. Insurance
> companies have checks and balances to prevent this but
> it still happens all too frequently.

YOUR STRATEGY
MAKE A CLAIM FOR POWER OUTAGE DAMAGE *IF* THE POWER LINE OR TRANSFORMER THAT CUTS OFF YOUR POWER IS DAMAGED ON YOUR PROPERTY.

When your power goes off you may need emergency power to keep your household running (GENERATOR RENTAL). If it stays off more than one day your food will spoil (FOOD SPOILAGE). Without power, your home may become unlivable (ADDITIONAL LIVING EXPENSE).   Your insurance coverage may apply—but it applies differently to each of these events.   For all claims where power outage causes damage, remember these three words:

ON YOUR PROPERTY!

Power outage damage is only covered by insurance if the *power line or transformer* that cuts off your power is damaged **ON YOUR PROPERTY**.

YOUR STRATEGY
REQUEST PAYMENT FOR THE PURCHASE OF A NEW GENERATOR INSTEAD OF RENTING ONE.

If you have lost power to your property (and the power line or transformer that cut off the power is *on your property*) you may want to consider purchasing or renting a portable electrical generator.

Obtain a written estimate of the cost to rent a generator, per day, versus the cost to purchase one. Show the adjuster you can save the company money (because it would cost the company more if you rented one). The adjuster may be willing to pay you the purchase price in lieu of the cost to rent—and you may get to keep the generator!

Understand that the insurance company does technically own the generator. So unless you can convince the adjuster to handle it this way, you must give up the generator to the insurance company—or buy it back as salvage.

YOUR STRATEGY
FOOD SPOILAGE IS NOT ALWAYS COVERED—BUT INCLUDE THE VALUE OF THE SPOILED FOOD IN YOUR CLAIM, IN CASE IT IS.

Not everyone has coverage for food spoilage. Listed here are two different situations which may illustrate whether you have coverage for food spoilage:

EXAMPLE #1: City generators shut down and your power goes off.

In example one, there is no food spoilage coverage. Why—because the power loss DID NOT OCCUR ON YOUR PROPERTY. It was the city generators that failed and the city generator is *not* on your property.

EXAMPLE #2: During the earthquake the (*chimney, tree, weather head, T.V. antenna mast, falling debris, anything)* knocked the power line down ON YOUR PROPERTY.

In example two, since the power interruption occurred ON YOUR PROPERTY, there is coverage for spoiled food.

Other than by a power outage on your property, there are three other instances when food spoilage may be covered after a disaster. They are:

1. **WHEN THE INSURANCE COMPANY VOLUNTARILY COVERS THE LOSS** as a good will gesture or in response to a request from the State Insurance Department.

2. **IF YOUR FREEZER OR REFRIGERATOR FELL OVER OR THE DOOR FLEW OPEN** in the earthquake.

3. **IF THE INSURANCE COMPANY PROVIDES "FOOD SPOILAGE" AS ADDITIONAL COVERAGE.** When this is the case, coverage is usually limited to $500.00 maximum.

Always include the value of spoiled food in your claim. Use the easy to follow form in the **CLAIM SIMPLI-FILER** or create your own. When you list food items, make the list detailed and complete. For example:

EXAMPLE OF A SPOILED FOOD LIST

1) 5 pounds of green tomatoes at 2.25 lb.   =11.25

2) 1 gal of milk at 2.35 gal.   = 2.35

3) 3 pounds of chuck roast at 1.89 lb.   = 5.67

4) 2 pounds of frying chickens at .99 lb.   = 1.98

5) 10 pounds of jumbo shrimp at 9.98 lb. =99.80

6) etc.

TOTAL LOSS OF FOOD SPOILED   =$X00.00

Power Surge Damage

Typically after a power outage, when the power is restored and turned back on, there is a power surge or spike that can cause damage to electronic equipment, motors and electrical appliances. A power surge is not damage caused by a power outage—so the *power line or transformer* that cuts off your power which generates the power surge does *not* have to be on your property. There is specific coverage under the homeowners policy to cover *some* of your personal property for damage caused by artificial electric currents (power surges). You generally have coverage for damage resulting from power surge for the following:

ITEMS GENERALLY COVERED FOR POWER SURGE

- **WASHERS AND DRYERS**

- **AIR CONDITIONERS AND FURNACES**

- **OVENS AND RANGES**

- **FANS AND ELECTRIC MOTORS**

- **REFRIGERATORS**

But you are generally NOT covered for damage resulting from power surge for:

ITEMS GENERALLY *NOT* COVERED FOR POWER SURGE

- COMPUTERS
- TELEVISIONS
- RADIOS
- VCR'S
- TUBES, TRANSISTORS OR SIMILAR ELECTRONIC COMPONENTS.

YOUR STRATEGY
USE SURGE PROTECTORS OR UNPLUG YOUR ELECTRONIC EQUIPMENT AFTER ANY POWER OUTAGE.

Power surge can do significant damage to your property and much of what gets damaged generally is not covered by insurance. Do not get caught believing your electronic equipment (personal computer, VCR, stereo, etc.) is covered for electrical damage, only to get your claim DENIED after a power surge.

If your power goes off for any reason, unplug all appliances and shut off all motors (including air conditioners) *before* the power comes back on! I also would recommend that you buy surge protectors for electronic equipment. Many surge protectors have warranties that cover power surge damage to connected equipment.

CHAPTER 9

REPLACEMENT COST COVERAGE AND DEPRECIATION

Even if you purchased replacement cost coverage, you still may have to deal with depreciation. Depreciation represents a deduction from the full replacement cost and is calculated based on the age and usage of the property. Simply stated: depreciation means loss in value.

YOUR STRATEGY
WATCH OUT FOR THE STRINGS ATTACHED TO REPLACEMENT COST COVERAGE.

Replacement cost coverage means you get the cost of new property to replace your used property. This applies to building repairs as well as replacement of contents. Easy enough, right?

Well, not exactly. Even if you have purchased replacement cost coverage for all or part of your property, NOT ALL COMPANIES WILL PAY YOU THE REPLACEMENT COST UP FRONT!

Many insurance companies deduct the depreciation from the settlement until the repairs or replacement are complete.

YOUR STRATEGY
ASK THE ADJUSTER WHETHER THE INSURANCE COMPANY PLANS TO TAKE "HOLDBACK DEPRECIATION."

You need to ask the adjuster whether the insurance company plans to take "holdback depreciation." If the insurance company does not "holdback," or if your claim is under $1000.00, you should get paid new for used on all items subject to replacement cost coverage. If the company does intend to "holdback," read on.

YOUR STRATEGY
UNDERSTAND HOW "HOLDBACK DEPRECIATION" WORKS *BEFORE* YOU SETTLE YOUR CLAIM.

The insurance company has the right to withhold the dollar difference between the actual cash value (the depreciated value of your used property) and the full replacement cost. Since the difference (the value of the depreciation) is withheld from you until you repair or replace, it is called "holdback depreciation." This dollar difference will be paid to you later *if* you do the repairs or replace the property *and* make a claim for the holdback within 180 days.

Holdback depreciation is a well kept secret. The subject of holdback doesn't usually come up during the claim adjusting process until the last few moments of signing the final paperwork and before you receive a check. The adjuster will say something like this:

"Here is the amount we agreed to Mrs. Doubtful, your total loss is $XX,000.00. The amount you will receive is $X,000.00 now and you can make a claim for the balance when you do the repairs and replace all the personal property you listed. Just submit the receipts to the company within 180 days . . . Oh, no one told you about holdback? Yeah, the insurance company has the right to hold the difference between the actual cash value and the full replacement cost until you repair or replace the items we agreed to in our settlement. You will be receiving the check for $X,000.00 within the next few weeks."

It is that quick. You agreed to settle your claim for one amount and now you hear that you are getting a check for significantly less—with strings attached before you can receive the difference. The insurance company has the right to take holdback—that's a given. But, you can *minimize* the holdback amount if you *negotiate* the depreciation.

YOUR STRATEGY
TAKE AN ASSERTIVE ROLE—MINIMIZE THE DEPRECIATION TO MAXIMIZE YOUR SETTLEMENT.

The insurance textbook method for calculating depreciation is by percentages. For example, a washing machine has as estimated life expectancy of ten years. After one year it has depreciated 10%, after two years—20%, and so on until the tenth year when it is 100% depreciated or its value has diminished to $0.00. Based on the textbook method, when the property is worn out or completely obsolete, it is considered fully depreciated or worthless.

So much for the textbook method. Depreciation is rarely—if ever—calculated this way. Believe it or not, adjusters usually pull percentages of depreciation out of thin air, sometimes not even knowing how old or used an item or building actually is. But they want you to believe there is a top secret, scientific calculation being used to decide depreciation on your property. Not hardly! There are no rules for depreciation. The reality is deductions for depreciation are arbitrary and made haphazardly. Therefore, deductions for depreciation are *completely* negotiable.

YOUR STRATEGY
ALWAYS ASK THE ADJUSTER—UP FRONT—WHAT ITEMS ARE SUBJECT TO DEPRECIATION AND HOLDBACK.

Because adjusters seldom tell you the amount of depreciation they are planning to take on your claim, always ask the adjuster to tell you which items are subject to depreciation. Then NEGOTIATE EACH ITEM INDIVIDUALLY!

Depreciation should be assessed on an item by item basis. No two items will age or wear out at the same rate. So, you *must* take an assertive role in the assessment of depreciation on your property! Only *you* will know the usefulness, age and how well your property has been maintained—so *you* decide what is a reasonable percentage of depreciation for each item—and STAND YOUR GROUND!

For example; block walls may be subject to depreciation, but how long do they really last (barring damage from an earthquake)? Any depreciation taken on block walls should be less than 10%—despite its age. If the adjuster wants to take more, ask the adjuster how long the pyramids have been standing. The point is, block walls won't be used up in our lifetime so the depreciation should be minimal.

YOUR STRATEGY
SEND A LETTER TO CONFIRM THAT YOU INTEND TO COLLECT YOUR "HOLDBACK."

You can collect the holdback when all the repairs and replacement are complete. Or you can claim holdback on each item as it is repaired or replaced. Just don't forget to complete the repairs and replace the items within 180 days of when the claim is officially closed. You should consider sending a certified letter to confirm your right to collect full replacement cost (the holdback amount) once the claim is concluded. The sample letter that follows can help you to do this:

Sample Letter for Claiming "Holdback"

XYZ Insurance Company
100 N. First Street
Los Angeles, California   09990

RE: Insured: Getmoore Later   April 12, 199X
       Date of Loss: 01-17-199X
       Policy#: 1290-121212
       Claim#: 123-456-788

CERTIFIED MAIL, RETURN RECEIPT REQUESTED

Attention: Holden Mimonie, Adjuster

Dear Mr. Mimonie,

I am making claim for full replacement cost and holdback depreciation. In doing so, I would like to know that I can make further claim should it be discovered that during such repair or replacement, the price for such repair or replacement has increased or that further damage is discovered that would increase the whole amount of this loss. Thank you.

Sincerely,

Getmoore Later

CHAPTER 10

HARDBALL NEGOTIATION STRATEGIES

Ideally, property insurance claims should be handled so that each claim is resolved promptly and all policyholders are treated equally and fairly and paid according to what is damaged. But this is not reality—especially after a disaster. So if you have made your claim to the insurance company, provided all reasonable documentation necessary, requested payment for your full entitlement and you are *still* getting the run-around or an unreasonable offer, it's time for HARDBALL!!! With "Hardball Negotiation Strategies," you will use all available means (short of hiring an attorney) to persuade the insurance company and the adjuster to negotiate with you in "good faith."

YOUR STRATEGY
DOCUMENT THE DIRT.

Take good notes of the adjuster's actions and conversations (missed meetings, failure to return phone calls, verbal claim denials, etc.) You need to have proof that the adjuster is treating you badly or unfairly.

Have your file or **CLAIM SIMPLI-FILER** ready for action. It should include the documentation of all inappropriate actions taken by the adjuster or insurance company. Proper documentation of certain inappropriate actions has resulted in adjusters and insurance companies being fined by the State Insurance Commissioner. An insurance company could even be in jeopardy of losing its license!

The insurance company owes you a high degree of good faith and fairness in all its business dealings with you. When the insurance company no longer treats you with good faith, by mishandling the claim or denying a claim that should be covered, you may have a separate claim for "breach of the implied covenant of good faith and fair dealing." Insurance companies (when they will speak of it) call this **"BAD FAITH."** In some states, separate claims of this type may allow you to collect amounts high enough (some have been in the millions) to punish the insurance company for its "Bad Faith."

Most states have laws dealing with how claims are to be handled by adjusters. If you feel you may be a victim of any of the following practices, you will want to document each act in your file or **CLAIM SIMPLI-FILER** to be used in your letters to the insurance company, State Insurance Department and for use by an attorney, if necessary.

The "Model Unfair Claims Practices Act" is summarized in the pages that follow. It became the model each state legislature modified and adopted. You should compare these rules with how your claim has *been* or is *being* handled.

THE MODEL UNFAIR CLAIMS PRACTICES ACT

1) **MISREPRESENTING PERTINENT FACTS OR INSURANCE POLICY PROVISIONS** relating to coverages at issue;

2) **FAILING TO ACKNOWLEDGE AND ACT REASONABLY PROMPTLY UPON COMMUNICATIONS** with respect to claims arising under insurance policies;

3) **FAILING TO ADOPT AND IMPLEMENT REASONABLE STANDARDS FOR THE PROMPT INVESTIGATION OF CLAIMS** arising under insurance policies;

4) **REFUSING TO PAY CLAIMS WITHOUT CONDUCTING A REASONABLE INVESTIGATION** based upon all available information;

5) **FAILING TO AFFIRM OR DENY COVERAGE FOR CLAIMS WITHIN A REASONABLE TIME** after proof of loss statements have been completed;

6) **NOT ATTEMPTING IN GOOD FAITH TO EFFECTUATE PROMPT, FAIR AND EQUITABLE SETTLEMENT OF CLAIMS** in which liability has become reasonably clear;

7) **COMPELLING INSUREDS TO SUE IN ORDER TO RECOVER AMOUNTS DUE UNDER AN INSURANCE POLICY BY OFFERING SUBSTANTIALLY LESS THAN THE AMOUNTS ULTIMATELY RECOVERED IN LAWSUITS** brought by such insureds;

8) **ATTEMPTING TO SETTLE A CLAIM FOR LESS THAN THE AMOUNT TO WHICH A REASONABLE MAN WOULD HAVE BELIEVED HE WAS ENTITLED** by reference to written or printed advertising material accompanying or made part of an application;

9) **ATTEMPTING TO SETTLE CLAIMS ON THE BASIS OF AN APPLICATION WHICH WAS ALTERED** without notice to, or knowledge or consent of, the insured;

10) MAKING CLAIM PAYMENTS TO INSUREDS OR BENEFICIARIES NOT ACCOMPANIED BY AN EXPLANATION describing the coverage under which the payments are being made;

11) MAKING KNOWN TO INSUREDS OR CLAIMANTS A POLICY OF APPEALING FROM ARBITRATION AWARDS IN FAVOR OF INSUREDS OR CLAIMANTS for the purpose of compelling them to accept settlements or compromises less than the amount awarded in arbitration;

12) DELAYING THE INVESTIGATION OR PAYMENT OF CLAIMS BY REQUIRING AN INSURED, CLAIMANT, OR THE PHYSICIAN OF EITHER TO SUBMIT A PRELIMINARY CLAIM REPORT and then requiring the subsequent submission of formal proof of loss forms, both of which submissions contain substantially the same information;

13) FAILING TO PROMPTLY SETTLE CLAIMS, WHERE THE LIABILITY HAS BECOME REASONABLY CLEAR, UNDER ONE PORTION OF THE INSURANCE POLICY COVERAGE in order to influence settlements under other portions of the insurance policy coverage;

14) FAILING TO PROVIDE A REASONABLE EXPLANATION OF THE BASIS IN THE INSURANCE POLICY IN RELATION TO THE FACTS OR APPLICABLE LAW FOR DENIAL OF A CLAIM or for the offer of a compromise settlement.

The following list of improper actions by the adjuster is provided to give you some idea of the type of behaviors you should document:

A LIST OF IMPROPER ACTIONS BY THE ADJUSTER

- **THE ADJUSTER INTENTIONALLY CONCEALS, TAMPERS WITH OR REARRANGES ANY PART OF YOUR CLAIM** to lower its value.

- **FAILURE BY THE ADJUSTER TO RESPOND** to your inquiries.

- **THE ADJUSTER DELAYS THE HANDLING OF THE CLAIM** to wear you down.

- **ANY ACTIVITY THAT WOULD CAUSE A REASONABLE PERSON TO OBSERVE "THEY SHOULDN'T BE ALLOWED TO GET AWAY WITH THAT!"**

- **ANY MISLEADING OR FALSE STATEMENTS** made by your adjuster when explaining coverages, conditions, or exclusions.

- **THE ADJUSTER DIDN'T GIVE YOU ENOUGH INFORMATION** to describe what was and was not being paid for.

- **ANY VIOLATION OF YOUR STATE'S VERSION OF THE MODEL "UNFAIR CLAIMS PRACTICES ACT."**

- **VIOLATION OF ANY OF YOUR STATE'S TIME LIMIT REQUIREMENTS.** (See summary of California's below.)

- **ANY DEROGATORY REFERENCES** regarding your religion, race, sexual preference, marital status, age or number of children, etc.

- **ANY CHALLENGE TO YOUR INTEGRITY THAT** is made without evidence.

There are other laws in many states that govern the handling of claims by insurance companies, agents and independent adjusters. Many of these laws contain time limits and other matters that may help you. These laws are not reproduced here and it is recommended that you contact an attorney or the State Insurance Department about how claims should be handled if you want an in depth review.

In California there are regulations that govern the handling of claims. This is referred to as the California Code of Regulations, Title 10, Chapter 5, Subchapter 7.5, Sections 2695.1-2695.17.

A summary of California's present time limits follows. You should measure the adjuster's performance against these time limits with regard to how your claim is handled.

SUMMARY OF CALIFORNIA'S TITLE 10 TIME LIMITS FOR HANDLING CLAIMS

ACTIVITY	CALENDAR DAYS (maximum times)
1. The Adjusters file must have proof that you were contacted.	15
2. Adjuster must provide to you any forms required.	15
3. Adjuster must have proof that a response was given to any inquiry from you.	15
4. Adjuster must accept or deny the claim after receiving your "proof of claim."	40
4b. If additional time is needed by the adjuster, that notice must be in writing.	(every) 30
5. Adjuster must tender the payment for claims not in dispute.	30
6. Adjuster must respond to any inquiry by the State Insurance Dept.	21

While I listed the deadlines in California, you should check to see if there are similar time limits in your state.

YOUR STRATEGY
TAPE RECORD YOUR CONVERSATIONS.

There are times when you will want to preserve the information given to you by the adjuster in a conversation—in person or over the telephone. Record it on a tape recorder. Adjusters are familiar with this process, but it is usually them recording you! There are inexpensive recording devices for telephones available at electronics stores if your conversation is not in person.

It will *always* be to your advantage to obtain permission before the tape begins. Simply turn on the recorder and ask for permission to record the conversation. An adjuster with nothing to hide should have no problem with you recording any conversation.

Once permission is obtained, proceed to identify yourself and have the adjuster identify him or herself on the recording. Next state the date, what time it is, and whether you are speaking from a telephone or in person. Ask all the questions you wish to have answered. A simple guide, **"QUESTIONS TO ASK DURING A RECORDED STATEMENT"** is included in the **CLAIM SIMPLI-FILER**. Make notes of what the adjuster said and save the tape in your file.

> **NOTE:** Check federal, state and local laws on telephone recording devices for possible use restrictions.

The Hardball Letters

With your documentation in order in your file or **CLAIM SIMPLI-FILER**, you are ready for action. The following letters should be written in progression until you get your intended result.

YOUR STRATEGY
GET THE INSURANCE COMPANY'S POSITION IN WRITING—LETTER #1.

You need to write a letter asking the adjuster to put the company's position in writing. The adjuster's response to your letter will confirm, in writing, specifically why the company is not paying your claim. This is also an opportunity for the adjuster to rethink your claim and do the right thing. It is okay to include any points of disagreement you already have identified. See the sample letter that follows:

Sample Letter To The Adjuster To Get The Insurance Company To State Its Position In Writing: Hardball Letter #1

XYZ Insurance Company
100 North First Street
Los Angeles, CA. 90000

RE: Insured: Ima Reelfair   Date: Dec. 19, 199X
         Date of Loss: 01-17-199X
         Policy#: 123-55-98 F
         Claim#: 456-89-129

CERTIFIED MAIL, RETURN RECEIPT REQUESTED

Attention: Mr. Don T. Wannapay, Adjuster

Dear Mr. Wannapay,

This letter concerns the discussions you and I have had recently concerning the earthquake loss to my home. I would like to know the insurance company's position on my claim as I don't understand why my claim hasn't already been paid in full.   Since coverage is not an issue, please answer the following:

1) WHAT else is expected from me before payment will be made, and

2) WHEN can I expect payment?

(*Amend the following paragraph to fit your situation*)
You have made only one offer to settle this claim for $X,000.00 and my estimate from a qualified contractor totals $XX,000.00. I also do not understand how you came up with the holdback depreciation you are taking on my claim.

I insist upon full compliance by your company with all state statutes relative to fair claims practices and any deadlines contained therein.

Please respond within ten working days. I am eager to resolve this matter. I would prefer to keep all further communications from you in writing.

Sincerely,

Ima Reelfair

YOUR STRATEGY
FIND OUT THE NAMES OF THE "RIGHT" PEOPLE.

Here is the most common claims management "chain of command." It begins with the **Catastrophe Office Supervisor** as the first supervisory level and ends with the **General Manager** or **C.E.O.** as the "top dog." Call the insurance company and obtain the names of the people in the following positions:

- The **Catastrophe Office Supervisor**
- The **Regional Claims Manager**
- The **Attorney** in charge of the legal department
- The **Vice President of Claims**
- The **General Manager** or C.E.O.

Put the names in your file or **CLAIM SIMPLI-FILER** for use in the next letter(s).

YOUR STRATEGY
COMPLAIN TO THE "RIGHT" PEOPLE—LETTER #2.

If your previous letter(s) didn't convince the adjuster to try to settle within the time limit you gave, then I guarantee some heads are going to roll if you send the next letter to any person on the "right" people list.

In a certified letter to the management of the insurance company, identify and document the actions of the adjuster that may qualify as unfair claims practices. In this letter you should conclude by threatening to ask the State Insurance Department to help you in getting the proper settlement.

You can start by sending a letter to the first person on the list and sending carbon copies to everyone else or you can send an original to each individual. The more "right" people involved in your complaint, the more responsive each person will be in the handling of your claim.

Send all letters by certified mail, return receipt requested. See the sample letter that follows:

Sample Letter To The Insurance Company Supervisor: Hardball Letter #2

XYZ Insurance Company
100 North First Street
Los Angeles, CA. 90090

RE: Insured: Betty Rethinksit   Date: December 19, 199X
     Date of Loss: 01-17-199X
     Policy number: 123-55-98 B
     Claim Number: 456-89-000

CERTIFIED MAIL, RETURN RECEIPT REQUESTED

Attention: Mr. Immen Trublnow, Catastrophe Office Supervisor

Dear Mr. Trublnow,

This letter is concerning the discussions your adjuster and I have had recently regarding the earthquake loss to my home. I have complied with all requests your company has made to date.

I gave notice of my claim to your company on (*insert date*). (*For California residents, add the following sentence.*) Please provide me a copy of proof that you have acknowledged my claim timely.

(*Amend the following paragraph to fit your situation. The sample paragraph used here is from a carpet claim. List all facts as they relate specifically to your claim. List all actions of the adjuster that could be unfair or inappropriate.*)

Your adjuster has made only one offer of $X,000.00 to settle this claim. My estimate from a qualified contractor total $XX,000.00. Your adjuster has not answered several telephone calls I have made to his office. He has told me to hire an attorney or demand an appraisal if I am unhappy with your offer. Your adjuster has told me that I could not have my carpet replaced, even though there are glass particles in it, unless I had small children. I feel this action is insensitive and discriminatory.

I insist upon your full compliance with all state laws that obligate you to deal fairly with me. You have refused to explain your position on my claim satisfactorily.

The only conclusion I can reach is that XYZ Insurance Company does not wish to deal with me in good faith. Due to the nature of the adjuster's actions, I am requesting a copy of that part of your claims manual detailing the procedure for handling my type of claim, including requirements for responding to complaints.

If I do not receive a reasonable explanation and reasonable offer by (*insert date for two weeks after the date you send the letter*), I will be forced to take further action regarding your company's apparent bad faith, including but not limited to, filing a complaint with the State Insurance Department.

Sincerely yours,

Betty Rethinksit

CC:

Boomin Biznis, XYZ Agent
Trien Forapromotion, XYZ Regional Claims Manager
Lea Gull, XYZ Attorney in Charge of the Legal Dept.
Goen Tobepeeved, XYZ Vice President of Claims
Whyme Whynow, XYZ General Manager

YOUR STRATEGY
COMPLAIN TO THE STATE INSURANCE DEPARTMENT—LETTER #3

Most adjusters are not as familiar as they should be with the state laws or the time limits, but they are all painfully aware of the possibility of having to respond to the State Insurance Department. If the previous letter(s) still didn't get you a satisfactory settlement, there will be hell to pay now! What is the insurance company's greatest dread? Answering inquires from the State Insurance Department!

When writing to the State Insurance Department, be sure to enclose copies of your previous letters and all other written documentation, estimates, etc. regarding your claim.

> **NOTE:** The addresses of the State Insurance
> Departments are found in the appendix.

A sample letter to the State Insurance Department follows:

Sample Letter To The State Insurance Department: Hardball Letter #3

California Department of Insurance
3450 Wilshire Blvd.
Los Angeles, CA. 90010

RE: Insured: Imso Sickofthis   Date: December 30, 199X
       Date of Loss: 01-17-199X
       Policy#: 123-55-98 B
       Claim#: 456-89-000
       Insurance Company: XYZ Insurance Company

CERTIFIED MAIL, RETURN RECEIPT REQUESTED

Attention: Claims Service Bureau, Consumer Complaints Dept.

To whom it may concern:

(*Amend the following paragraph to fit your situation. List all evidence of potential "bad faith" or adjuster actions that you have documented.*) I had an earthquake loss to my home on 09-17-199X and after numerous discussions with the adjuster, Mr. Don T. Wannapay, I have been unable to get him to answer my calls and discuss my claim.

Mr. Wannapay has stated that my roof and interior walls are repairable for $X,000.00 and I have a contractor's written opinion stating that because of the cracks, my plaster walls must be completely torn out and replaced. Including the necessary roof repairs, I have a total claim of $XX,000.00. I do not believe this claim is being handled timely or in good faith and would appreciate your review and assistance.

I enclose copies of all my correspondence with XYZ Insurance Company as well as estimates from my contractor. Thank you for your assistance.

If you find this claim was not handled properly according to the Insurance Department guidelines and applicable laws, I request that the insurance company not only pay the full amount of the claim, but also be required to pay interest on the amount of the claim not previously paid. I would further request your office sanction the insurance company as you deem appropriate under the circumstances.

Sincerely,

Imso Sickofthis

Allow time for the State Insurance Department to complete an investigation. The amount of time the investigation takes will vary from case to case. Within one or two weeks, there should be a representative from the Insurance Commissioner's office assigned to your claim and who will be responding to your complaint letter.

You can still settle your claim at any time. If you do not get any satisfaction from the State Insurance Department, your options are: invoking the Appraisal Clause (see the chapter "The Appraisal Clause") or hiring an attorney to represent you.

Remember, ALWAYS KEEP COPIES of correspondence in your file or **CLAIM SIMPLI-FILER**.

CHAPTER **11**

THE APPRAISAL CLAUSE

The appraisal clause is a way to resolve an impasse between you and your insurance company over the *amount* of your loss—but not coverage problems or coverage denials. The decision as to what your claim is worth is no longer decided by you or the insurance company. That decision is made by two appraisers—if they can agree. If they cannot agree, the appraisers then hire someone to act as an umpire. The umpire then decides what your claim is worth.

The appraisal clause is by no means a hammer or strategy for you to use—it is the way the *policy* provides to resolve disputes. If you have tried every other possible method and have been unsuccessful at resolving your impasse with the insurance company (including the use of "Hardball" Negotiations), then it may be necessary to use the appraisal clause to resolve your dispute.

Let me caution you—appraisal is *supposed* to be an "impartial" process. In reality, insurance companies always try to stack the deck. The insurance company will select an appraiser who regularly handles its claims and/or appraisals and that appraiser will "recommend" an umpire who usually wants business from the insurance company. Get the picture?

YOU DO NOT WANT AN UMPIRE WHO WAS EITHER AN APPRAISER BEFORE OR HAS AN INTEREST IN GETTING ANY BUSINESS AT ALL FROM THE INSURANCE COMPANY! It is simply unfair to you.

There are no guarantees of a favorable outcome—but if you "go to appraisal," you may be able to neutralize the advantage the insurance company has by carefully selecting your appraiser and umpire. The appraisal clause is found in the **CONDITIONS** portion of business and homeowners type policies. Usually the way the process works is as follows:

THE BASIC APPRAISAL CLAUSE PROCESS

1. **EITHER YOU OR THE INSURANCE COMPANY MAKES A WRITTEN DEMAND FOR APPRAISAL.**

2. **WITHIN TWENTY (20) DAYS AFTER RECEIPT OF THE WRITTEN DEMAND, EACH PARTY SHALL SELECT A COMPETENT, INDEPENDENT APPRAISER.**

3. **THE TWO APPRAISERS WILL CHOOSE AN IMPARTIAL UMPIRE.**

4. **IF THE INDEPENDENT APPRAISERS CANNOT AGREE UPON AN UMPIRE WITHIN (15) DAYS, YOU OR YOUR INSURANCE COMPANY MAY REQUEST A JUDGE OF A COURT OF RECORD IN YOUR STATE TO SELECT AN UMPIRE.**

5. **THE APPRAISERS WILL SEPARATELY CALCULATE THE LOSS.**

6. **IF THE APPRAISERS AGREE ON THE AMOUNT OF THE LOSS, THEIR DECISION WILL BE FINAL.**

7. **IF THE APPRAISERS FAIL TO AGREE, THEY WILL SUBMIT THEIR DIFFERENCES TO THE UMPIRE.**

8. **WRITTEN AGREEMENT BY ANY TWO OF THESE THREE PEOPLE SHALL SET THE AMOUNT OF THE LOSS.**

9. **EACH APPRAISER SHALL BE PAID BY THE PARTY SELECTING THAT APPRAISER.**

10. **OTHER EXPENSES OF THE APPRAISAL AND THE COMPENSATION OF THE UMPIRE SHALL BE SHARED EQUALLY.**

YOUR STRATEGY
NOTIFY THE INSURANCE COMPANY IN WRITING THAT YOU WANT TO "GO TO APPRAISAL. "

If the time comes to use the appraisal clause, you will need to notify the company, in writing, that you want to go to appraisal. There are no "standard" forms that must be filled out—so don't let them tell you otherwise. All you need to do is notify the insurance company in writing.

Here is a sample notification letter:

Sample Appraisal Notification Letter

XYZ Insurance Company
100 North First Street
Los Angeles, CA. 90000

RE:　　Insured: Haddy Nuff　　　　　　Date: July 1, 199X
　　　　Date of Loss: 01-17-199X
　　　　Policy#: 123-55-98 C
　　　　Claim#: 456-89-090

CERTIFIED MAIL, RETURN RECEIPT REQUESTED

Attention: Mr. Toetal Impasse, Adjuster

Dear Sir,

(Amend the following paragraphs to fit your situation.)
This is to inform you I do not agree with patching and painting the earthquake damage to my walls and ceiling as a method of repair. I also disagree with the payment to only shampoo my carpets as a method to deodorize, remove mildew and mud stains due to the water damage from broken water pipes in the living room and hallway.

According to the appraisal provision of my policy, I hereby make demand for an appraisal and name Harry Hardball, 123 Pennyblossom Lane, Santa Monica, California 99999, as my appraiser. I insist upon full compliance by your company with all state statutes relative to fair claims practices and any deadlines contained therein. Please notify me of the name of your appraiser not later than twenty (20) days from the date of this letter so our two appraisers may proceed.

Sincerely,

Haddy Nuff

YOUR STRATEGY
SELECT AN APPRAISER.

You need to select someone to be your appraiser. Most people will select the general contractor or roofer who has already inspected the damage and has first hand knowledge of the claim. This person will usually handle the appraisal without additional costs.

YOUR STRATEGY
MATCH CREDENTIALS OF THE INSURANCE COMPANY'S APPRAISER.

If the opportunity presents itself, you will want to match the credentials of your appraiser with that of the insurance company's appraiser—"trade for trade." If the insurance company selects a roofer, you select one too. If the insurance company selects an engineer, you may want to select one as well.

If the insurance company selects a consulting engineer, and you have already selected someone with fewer credentials you may be at a disadvantage. There is nothing in the policy about changing appraisers—so you should be able to name another appraiser with matching or better credentials.

> **Note:** If you use an engineer as an appraiser, the services can cost anywhere from $85.00 to $150.00 per hour. On an average claim, an appraisal by an engineer can cost $200.00-$800.00.

YOUR STRATEGY
HELP THE APPRAISER PREPARE THE APPRAISAL REPORT.

Once you have selected your appraiser, don't be afraid to help in the preparation of the appraisal. Review—with your appraiser—all your damage. Don't leave anything out. You and the appraiser should agree on the cause of damage, the extent of damage, and the costs of repairs *before* the appraiser represents you in the appraisal process.

YOUR APPRAISER'S REPORT SHOULD:

1. **LIST ALL YOUR DAMAGE AND WHAT IT WILL COST TO MAKE REPAIRS.**

2. **CONFIRM THE CAUSE OF THE DAMAGE.**

3. **EXPLAIN WHY THE EXTENT OF REPAIRS ARE NECESSARY.**

If your appraiser is unable to reach agreement with the opposing appraiser on the cost and extent of the damage, (which is often the case), the differences must be submitted to an umpire. The appraiser should then add to the appraisal:

4. **A FULL LIST IDENTIFYING ALL THE DIFFERENCES (COSTS, EXTENT OF DAMAGE, ETC.) BETWEEN THE TWO APPRAISALS.**

It is essential for your appraiser to list the differences between the two appraisals, or these differences may not be evaluated by the umpire.

YOUR STRATEGY
SUGGEST UMPIRES WHO HAVE NO INTEREST IN OBTAINING INSURANCE CONSTRUCTION OR CONSULTING WORK.

Each appraiser submits a list of three potential umpires to the other. The two appraisers will try to agree on an umpire from the list of six choices. It is imperative that *you* are involved in the selection of the three potential umpires that your appraiser names!

Choose your potential umpires wisely. There is *no* requirement that the umpire visit the premises to inspect the damage! There is *no* requirement that the umpire know anything about repairs, construction, or insurance! The only qualification is that the umpire be impartial. I would add that it wouldn't hurt if your selections are respected and educated members of society—attorneys, chiropractors, dentists, school teachers, police officers, etc.

Make sure the three people you recommend are *willing* to act as an umpire. An average umpire's fee is between $100.00-$300.00 (but, like anything else, it is negotiable!) You and the insurance company must split the umpire's fee.

The insurance company will be at an advantage if your appraiser selects *any* of the company's choices for umpire. So tell your appraiser *not* to accept any umpire suggested by the insurance company's appraiser—period! If the insurance company's appraiser won't pick from your appraiser's list of potential umpires, then a judge must select the umpire.

YOUR STRATEGY
HAVE THE UMPIRE SWEAR—IN WRITING—TO BE IMPARTIAL.

Despite who is selected to act as the umpire, you should *insist* that the umpire sign a pledge to be impartial.   You can use the sample "Pledge of Impartiality" that follows:

> **NOTE:** If the insurance company refuses to allow this, contact an attorney for advice. This could be an attempt by the insurance company to unfairly "stack the deck."

PLEDGE OF IMPARTIALITY

I, the undersigned, swear and state that I have not previously acted in any capacity as an appraiser pursuant to the appraisal provisions contained in any policy of insurance. I further state that I have no financial interest in construction, consulting, or claims adjusting work for_____insurance company.

I understand that I may request any document, photograph, statement, or interview reasonably necessary to help me make an impartial decision.

I understand that I may inspect the property and the damage at issue, if necessary, to arrive at a decision.

Umpire_____

Notary Public_____

Subscribed and Sworn
to me on_____

That is all there is to the appraisal clause and process. Just remember these important points:

- **THE DECISION IS GENERALLY FINAL AND BINDING.**

- **YOU LOSE CONTROL OF THE NEGOTIATIONS AND OUTCOME.**

- **IT CAN TAKE WEEKS OR MONTHS FOR THE PLAYERS TO COMPLETE THE APPRAISAL PROCESS AND TO REACH A DECISION.**

- **ONLY GO TO APPRAISAL TO RESOLVE THE ITEMS IN DISPUTE, *NOT* THE ENTIRE CLAIM.**

It is my suggestion that you try all other strategies mentioned throughout the book *before* using the "Appraisal Clause."

CHAPTER 12

IF PART OF YOUR CLAIM IS DENIED

Sometimes denying part of your claim is appropriate, and sometimes it isn't. A denial on any part of your claim is reason enough to read this chapter.

Most denials are made verbally. You ask for payment for something, the adjuster says it's not covered—that is a partial denial. There are also instances where coverage is limited, which is usually stated verbally—and that too is a partial denial.

YOUR STRATEGY
DON'T MAKE YOUR CLAIM VERBALLY—MAKE YOUR CLAIM IN WRITING.

You want to avoid *verbal* denials, so make your claim in writing. If you want to be paid for food spoilage, don't ask over the phone. Put the claim in writing. If you want to be paid for your awnings, pool, driveway, patio, swing set, or *anything*—put your claim in writing.

I am not saying you will be paid for everything you claim in writing—it's just *less* likely you will be improperly denied for things that *are* covered! Easy-to-use forms to present your claim in writing are included in the **CLAIM SIMPLI-FILER**.

YOUR STRATEGY
MAKE THE ADJUSTER SHOW—IN WRITING—ANY EXCLUSIONS OR LIMITATIONS IN YOUR POLICY.

Do *not* accept an adjuster's word that there is no coverage or that there are other limitations or exclusions that apply to your claim. Make the adjuster respond with the company's position in writing on every item you claim. Request a copy of the appropriate part of the policy—highlighted—upon which the denial or limitation is based. If the adjuster cannot show you the policy provision that clearly supports the adjuster's position, then your claim may have been improperly denied or limited.

It is not only important to know what part of the policy the adjuster is relying upon, but also upon what *evidence* (documentation) the adjuster is basing the denial or limitation. (For example, stating that your cracked foundation is *not* due to the earthquake.) An adjuster's *opinion* is not enough to support a partial denial of your claim. Only if the adjuster can provide—to your satisfaction—the information to support the partial denial or the limitation, is the denial likely to be appropriate.

YOUR STRATEGY
IF THE ADJUSTER CANNOT SHOW YOU THE REASONS FOR THE PARTIAL DENIAL OR LIMITATION—IN WRITING— THEN CHALLENGE THE DECISION.

If the adjuster cannot put the reasons for the partial denial or limitation, in writing, then challenge the appropriateness of the denial. The best way to challenge the adjuster's decision is to write a letter, sent by certified mail, to the "right" people. (Regional Claims Manager is a great place to start!) Be specific in your letter by documenting the dates the adjuster called and the topics you discussed.

Here is a sample letter:

Sample Letter to Challenge A Denial

XYZ Insurance Company
100 North First Street
Los Angeles, CA. 90000

RE: Insured: Bee Phairtome   Date: 04-28-199X
        Date of Loss: 01-17-199X
        Policy number#: 123-55-98 D
        Claim Number#: 456-89-004

CERTIFIED MAIL, RETURN RECEIPT REQUESTED

Attention: Mr. Trien Forapromotion, Regional Claims Manager

Dear Mr. Forapromotion,
(Amend the paragraphs to fit your situation)
I advised my agent of my claim on 01-18-199X and again on 02-18-199X. I didn't receive a telephone call from Ms. Knot Hermoney, the adjuster, until five weeks after I turned in my claim. She came to my home on 03-27-199X and spent only a few minutes inspecting my damage. She didn't inspect and measure all the rooms that had damage, even after I told her where the damage was. I have provided all the documents she requested.

I received a phone call on 04-27-199X from Ms. Hermoney denying the claim for my *(carpet, spoiled food, pool, fence, personal property etc.)*   Her explanation was confusing and inadequate since I cannot understand the basis for the withholding of payment on my property. Furthermore, she didn't reserve any right to deny this part of my claim and I believe that right has been waived. I believe coverage does exist for this property and I expect payment by *(two weeks from the date of this letter)* for $X,000.00. I am requesting that your company comply with all its obligations under the policy.
Sincerely,

Bee Phairtome

YOUR STRATEGY
WRITE TO THE INSURANCE COMPANY'S LEGAL DEPARTMENT FOR THE COMPANY'S POSITION ON YOUR CLAIM.

The ultimate authority for what your policy says is a jury or judge—but there are a couple more strategies to try before hiring an attorney and suing the company. If you receive an inadequate response to your first letter, next you should consider writing to the insurance company's legal department.

Most insurance companies have legal departments that can *independently* pass judgment on grey areas of coverage. Legal departments are painfully aware of the high jury verdicts in "bad faith" cases—and they know many "bad faith" cases come from improper denials of coverage! So, legal departments do try *very hard* to see that coverage denials are accurate—it's their job.

Add to the letter anything that has occurred on your claim since you last wrote to the insurance company. List any time limits missed by the adjuster. Also, ask for a copy of the "Company Claims Manual" which deals with how your claim is *supposed* to be handled. This will raise the hair on the back of their necks! By asking for the claims manual, you are implying that you *intend to see* if the insurance company followed its own procedures on your claim! Not to follow its own procedure may be considered evidence of "bad faith." If you have to sue the insurance company, an attorney may be able to force the insurance company to give you a copy of the "Claims Manual"—and the legal department knows it!

Here is a sample letter:

Sample Letter To The Legal Department Regarding A Coverage Denial

XYZ Insurance Company
100 North First Street
Los Angeles, CA. 90090

RE: Insured: Willy Reconsidur   Date: 04-12-199X
        Date of Loss: 01-17-199X
        Policy #: 123-55-98 D
        Claim #: 456-89-004

CERTIFIED MAIL, RETURN RECEIPT REQUESTED

Attn: Ms. Lea Gull, Attorney in charge of the Legal Department

Dear Ms. Gull,

(Amend the following paragraphs to fit your situation)
I advised my agent of my claim on 01-18-199X. Four weeks later, on 02-18-199X, I received the first contact via telephone call from the adjuster, Mr. Don T. Wannapay. He came to my home on 02-27-199X to inspect my damage, spending only a few minutes. He didn't inspect and measure all the rooms that had damage, even after I told him where the damage was. I provided all the documents he requested at the time of our meeting.

I received his letter denying that part of my claim pertaining to my (*carpet, spoiled food, pool, fence, personal property etc.*). His explanation is confusing and inadequate since I cannot understand the basis for the withholding of payment on my property. Furthermore, he didn't reserve any right to deny this part of my claim and I believe that right has been waived.

IF PART OF YOUR CLAIM IS DENIED

I believe coverage does exist for this property and request payment by (*two weeks from the date of this letter*) for $X,000.00 (*always state the full amount you want to be paid*).

I received an unsatisfactory response to my letter of 03-28-199X to Mr. Wannapay's supervisor, Mr. Trien Forapromotion. In Mr. Forapromotion's response, he didn't address Mr. Wannapays improper handling of my claim (*list all time limit violations and improper adjuster actions*).

We are $X,000.00 apart from settling this claim. I am requesting that your company comply with all its obligations under the policy. If we cannot resolve this matter in the next ten days, I will request help from the State Insurance Department.

Due to the nature of the adjusters actions and the lack of adequate explanation from his supervisor, I am requesting a copy of that part of your claims manual detailing the procedure for handling my type of claim. Be sure to include the procedures to deny claims.

Sincerely,

Willy Reconsidur

cc:

Mr. Goen Tobepeeved, Vice President of Claims, XYZ Ins. Co.
Mr. Whyme Whynow, General Manager, XYZ Ins. Co.
State Insurance Department, (optional at this point)

YOUR STRATEGY

IF THE INSURANCE COMPANY'S LEGAL DEPARTMENT SAYS "NO COVERAGE," WRITE TO THE STATE INSURANCE DEPARTMENT.

If you still feel certain that you are improperly being denied coverage, write to the State Insurance Department for an investigation into your claim. Send copies of all the prior correspondence between you and the insurance company and state clearly why you believe your claim should be covered. Here is a sample letter:

Sample Letter Asking The State Insurance Department To Investigate A Coverage Denial

California Department of Insurance
3450 Wilshire Blvd.
Los Angeles, CA. 90010

RE: Insured: Rawngly D. Nyed   Date: 04-25-199X
       Date of Loss: 01-17-199X
       Policy number: 123-55-98 B
       Claim Number: 456-89-000
       Insurance Company: XYZ Insurance Company

Attention: Claims Service Bureau

To whom it may concern:

(Amend the following paragraphs to fit your situation. List all evidence of potential "bad faith" or inappropriate actions by the adjuster that you have documented.)

I advised my agent of my claim on 01-18-199X and again on 02-18-199X. I didn't receive a telephone call from Ms. Knot Hermoney, the adjuster, until five weeks after I turned in my claim. She came to my home on 02-27-199X and spent only a few minutes inspecting my damage. She didn't inspect and measure all the rooms that had damage, even after I told her where the damage was. I have provided all the documents she requested.

I received a phone call on 03-27-199X from Ms. Hermoney denying the claim for my (*carpet, spoiled food, pool, fence, personal property etc.*) Her explanation was confusing and inadequate since I cannot understand the basis for the withholding of payment on my claim. Furthermore, she didn't reserve any right to deny this part of my claim and I believe that right has been waived.

I have written to the insurance company and have not received an adequate explanation. We are $X,000.00 apart from settling this claim. I do not believe this claim was handled timely or in good faith and would appreciate your review.

If you find this claim was not handled properly according to the Insurance Department guidelines and applicable laws, I request that the insurance company not only pay the full amount of the claim, but also be required to pay interest on the amount of the claim not previously paid. I would further request your office sanction the insurance company as you deem appropriate under the circumstances.

Sincerely,

Rawngly D. Nyed

cc:

Mr. Goen Tobepeeved, Vice President of Claims, XYZ Ins. Co.
Mr. Whyme Whynow, General Manager, XYZ Ins. Co.
Ms. Lea Gull, Legal Dept., XYZ Insurance Co.

Enclosures:

All prior correspondence with XYZ Ins. Co.
The adjuster's estimate
The contractor's estimate

YOUR STRATEGY
WHEN COVERAGE IS NOT CLEAR BECAUSE IT IS "AMBIGUOUS," THE LAW WILL DECIDE COVERAGE IN YOUR FAVOR!

Whether you have coverage for something is not always black or white. There are occasionally "grey" areas or "ambiguities" in your policy (unclear terms that are confusing and subject to different interpretations). The good news is if the coverage is not clear the law will decide coverage in *your* favor—the bad news is most adjusters have a hard time admitting that coverage is not clear. If the adjuster cannot show you specifically in the policy and clearly explain why something is not covered, you may have a policy "ambiguity."

For example, you learned in earlier chapters, that pet boarding is covered as an additional living expense. So you ask the adjuster for money to pay for pet boarding for your pet goat while you are out of your home during the repair process. Chuckling, the adjuster says something like, "I am sorry, *they* don't cover goats." And you say, "Oh? Why don't you show me where pet boarding for goats is specifically excluded in my policy please?" The adjuster says, "Sure," and begins flipping through your policy.

After several minutes of searching the adjuster says, frustrated, "Well I can't seem to find it, but *they* have never (he means *he* has never) covered goats before so I am pretty sure it's *not* covered." And you say, "Since you can't show me the specific exclusion in the policy that excludes a goat as a pet, and you have denied me coverage in spite of that fact, I want a WRITTEN COVERAGE OPINION from the insurance company."

Most adjusters don't have the authority to deny claims without a supervisor's permission—though they verbally deny claims without permission on a regular basis! So when you ask for a written coverage opinion from the insurance company, the adjuster knows that the denial had *better* be right—or he or she is in *big* trouble. Now would be the time for the adjuster to back off the prior position to make darn sure the denial was proper.

If the adjuster submits your claim to a supervisor or the legal department for a coverage opinion, the adjuster will want you to *believe* you have no say in the outcome of this "coverage question." Not so! You have a right to know what is unclear about the coverage and you should state *your* opinion in writing. It will make it more difficult to deny your claim if the company is aware that you believe the wording in the policy is "ambiguous." You should consider writing a letter to the "right people." A sample letter follows:

Sample Letter When Coverage Is Unclear (Ambiguous Wording Or "Grey Area")

XYZ Insurance Company
100 North First Street
Los Angeles, CA. 90090

RE: Insured: Willy Denighme   Date: 04-28-199X
         Date of Loss: 01-17-199X
         Policy #: 123-55-98 B
         Claim #: 456-89-000

CERTIFIED MAIL, RETURN RECEIPT REQUESTED

Attention: Mr. Trien Forapromotion, Regional Claims Manager

Dear Mr. Forapromotion,
(Amend the following paragraphs to fit your situation)
I advised my agent of my claim on 01-18-199X. My first contact from your adjuster was on 02-08-199X and he came to my home on 02-27-199X to inspect my damage. The adjuster told me on 03-16-199X that coverage would not be provided for boarding my pet goat. He has not reserved any right to deny this part of my claim and I believe that right has been waived. Since he was unable to specifically point out the policy language that excludes coverage for a goat as a pet, this is obviously a "grey area."

I believe coverage does exist. I understand that should the matter be heard in a court of law, it is likely any ambiguities would be found in my favor. I am therefore, requesting that you reconsider your adjuster's denial and comply with all your obligations under the policy. I expect payment by *(two weeks from date of letter)* for $X00.00.

Sincerely,

Willy Denighme

CHAPTER 13

WHEN TO SETTLE YOUR CLAIM

Let me explain the term "settle." **"Settle" means you agree with the adjuster on the specific amount of money you are entitled to be paid for your claim**.

You are led to believe that the best settlement is a fast settlement—and it sure is—for the insurance company! The quicker the insurance company can get your claim settled, the less time you have to think about your damage, question your entitlement, or talk to your neighbors about what they are being paid by *their* insurance companies. It is great to receive money right away, but make it an "advance" or partial payment. Only when you have been made aware of everything you are entitled to collect, can you judge if your settlement offer is fair.

YOUR STRATEGY
IF YOU RECEIVE A SETTLEMENT CHECK IN THE MAIL AND YOU DIDN'T EVEN KNOW YOUR CLAIM WAS "SETTLED"—REQUEST A NEW ADJUSTER.

There are adjusters who run through claims at lightening speed, dummy up reports stating you *agreed* to a settlement and are "out of town before daybreak." These adjusters don't care what you are paid as long they receive their fee and "close" your file. Luckily, they are easy to spot. You will probably receive a settlement check in the mail without having agreed to the settlement. If this is your situation, call *and* write to the insurance company immediately. The following sample letter will put the insurance company on notice that your claim is *not* closed:

> **Note:** There is no need to send back the claim check. BUT—do not deposit the payment until the insurance company agrees, in writing, that the claim check is only a *partial* payment.

Sample Letter To Request
A New Adjuster

XYZ Insurance Company
100 N. First Street
Los Angeles, CA   90000

RE: Insured: Shirley Yorkiding   Date: 03-10-199X
       Date of Loss: 01-17-199X
       Policy#: 1290-121212
       Claim#: 123-456-787

Attention: Supervisor of Joe Noshow, Independent Adjuster

Dear Sir;

(Amend the following paragraph to fit your situation)
Mr. Noshow inspected my home, without an appointment, on 01-30-199X. I have not heard from Mr. Noshow since that date. I received a check in the mail today for $X,000.00 for final settlement on my claim. I am putting you on notice that I do not accept this amount as a final settlement.

I cannot work with anyone who treats me this way or is unwilling to discuss my claim in good faith.   Please advise me when a new adjuster is assigned.

Sincerely,

Shirley Yorkiding

CC: (your insurance agent)

YOUR STRATEGY
TRY TO SETTLE YOUR CLAIM BETWEEN THE 6TH AND 14TH WEEK FOLLOWING THE EARTHQUAKE.

There is generally a good and bad time to get an agreed settlement and to get your claim paid. Sometime within the 4th-6th week after the earthquake is a good time to begin the settlement process and anytime after 14 weeks may be a little too late.

REASONS NOT TO RUSH TO AN EARLY SETTLEMENT:

- **PRICES FOR BUILDING MATERIAL AND LABOR BEGIN TO GO UP** due to high demand. If your claim is settled too early, it is very likely you will receive less money for the actual costs of materials and labor.

- **AFTER SHOCKS CONTINUE TO EXPOSE HIDDEN DAMAGE.**

- **IT TAKES TIME TO GET ESTIMATES** and obtain the replacement cost of damaged personal property.

- **ANY NEW DAMAGE FROM AFTER SHOCKS BEYOND 72 HOURS AFTER THE INITIAL EARTHQUAKE WILL BE CONSIDERED A NEW LOSS** with another killer deductible.

- **ADDITIONAL LIVING EXPENSE COSTS MAY CHANGE AND/OR INCREASE.**

- **CONTRACTORS ARE TOO BUSY** and may not have the time in the first few weeks to accurately access your damage.

- **YOU NEED TO GET OVER THE SHOCK OF THE EARTHQUAKE** so you can make unemotional and informed decisions.

146

REASONS TO HAVE YOUR CLAIM SETTLED APPROXIMATELY 6 TO 14 WEEKS AFTER THE EARTHQUAKE:

- **ADJUSTERS ARE EAGER** to get out from under the many losses they have to handle so they are more willing to cooperate.

- **ADJUSTERS AND INSURANCE COMPANIES ARE SWAMPED.** They must pick their fights carefully. The insurance company may be too busy to argue about your claim—it may be all it can do just to print and mail checks. There is no way to pour over claims and review adjusters' work like it normally does.

- **YOU'VE HAD TIME TO GET INFORMED AND BE PREPARED.**

REASONS NOT TO HAVE YOUR CLAIM SETTLED BEYOND THE 14TH WEEK AFTER THE EARTHQUAKE:

- **THE INSURANCE COMPANIES BEGIN TO RECOGNIZE HOW MUCH MONEY THEY HAVE ALREADY PAID OUT.** If the disaster is large enough, senior management may fear financial instability for the company and individual job security for themselves. The obvious choice is to reduce "unnecessary" claim expenses.

- **INSURANCE COMPANIES TELL THE ADJUSTERS TO "TIGHTEN" THEIR ESTIMATES** on claims and try to carry out all the quality control standards (ways to reduce claim expenses) that they overlooked shortly after the earthquake.

An exception to these rules is if your home is a total loss. If that is your situation, settle your claim as soon as you feel confident that you are getting all that you are entitled to collect from your insurance policy.

YOUR STRATEGY
ACCEPT PARTIAL PAYMENTS TOWARD THE "FINAL" SETTLEMENT.

There is a better option other than a "one check" settlement. You can receive payment for one portion of your claim at a time. For example, you and the adjuster agree on the amount of damage to your garage but haven't agreed on the amount of damage to your home. Your insurance company is aware that any undisputed amount of your claim must be paid to you on request—so make the request for the agreed amount for the damage to your garage. It doesn't mean the *entire* claim is settled, just a portion of the claim.

This is particularly useful when there is a stalemate between you and the insurance company on the *final* amount you are owed. By receiving the undisputed amount, you can neutralize the company's tactic of holding all your claim money to force you to settle at its last offer.

Bottom line—other than advance payments, get prepared to begin receiving payment on your claim in about six weeks. But don't settle on the *final* amount of your claim until you agree with the adjuster on the specific amount of money you are entitled to be paid. It is not necessary to receive the claim payment in "one" final check. You can receive many checks that will add up to the "final" amount of the claim.

CHAPTER 14

REOPENING YOUR "CLOSED" CLAIM

Once the insurance company makes the "final" payment and declares your file "closed", it doesn't want to hear from you again. But hear from you again it should, if you are entitled to additional money!

Even if your claim was already paid some time ago, it would benefit you to review all the strategies in this book in light of what you were paid. When you find that you weren't paid for something and you know you should have been, reopen the claim.

Claims are easily reopened. You call or write the company—it's reopened. I've listed some of the common reasons to reopen your claim. The list does not, by any means, represents all the possible reasons your claim should be reopened or reinspected.

COMMON REASONS TO REOPEN YOUR CLAIM

- **THE ADJUSTER WORKED YOUR CLAIM TOO QUICKLY** and left out necessary repairs.

- **YOU DISCOVER NEW CRACKS** in your walls, ceiling or floor.

- **THE INSURANCE COMPANY DIDN'T PAY ENOUGH TO GET THE REPAIRS DONE.**

- **YOU HAVE ADDITIONAL LIVING EXPENSES** because the repairs are making your home unlivable.

- **YOU OR YOUR CONTRACTOR DISCOVER HIDDEN DAMAGE** which was not included in the original estimate.

- **YOU WERE ONLY PAID FOR HALF OF YOUR BLOCK WALLS OR FENCES** and you are the sole owner.

- **YOU REMEMBERED ADDITIONAL CONTENTS** that were not claimed but were damaged or lost in the earthquake.

- **YOU DISCOVER YOUR FLOORS, WINDOWS OR DOORS ARE UNEVEN.**

- **YOU WERE NOT PAID FOR SALES TAX AND DELIVERY** for replacing your personal property.

- **YOU ARE REQUESTING THE "HOLDBACK DEPRECIATION"** because you have replaced all or part of your personal property or completed your repairs.

- **PROFIT AND OVERHEAD WERE NOT INCLUDED** in your claim payment.

- **YOU BOUGHT GUARANTEED REPLACEMENT COST COVERAGE AND WERE TOLD IT DID NOT APPLY** to your garage or sheds.

- **AFTER READING THIS BOOK, YOU FIND OTHER ITEMS YOU DID NOT CLAIM** for which you believe you are owed payment.

First, call the insurance company. State the facts as you know them explaining the specific reason(s) you believe you are entitled to more money. Ask that someone come out to reinspect your property. After an earthquake, the insurance company will be reopening claims and doing reinspections for months to come so adding another to the list should not be a problem. Prepare for the reinspection just as you would on a new claim. Arrange for a contractor's estimate in advance. Have the contractor meet with the adjuster and follow the appropriate strategies listed throughout the book. If you do not get a quick response, consider modifying one of the following letters—send it by certified mail:

Sample Letter To Request A Reinspection
Of Your Claim

XYZ Insurance Company
100 North First Street
Sacramento, California 90000

RE: Insured: Ineeda Moore   Date: 04-27-199X
       Date of Loss: 01-17-199X
       Policy #: 123-45-98 A
       Claim #: 456-85-006

CERTIFIED MAIL, RETURN RECEIPT REQUESTED

Attention: Mr. Stressed Tothemax, Catastrophe Supervisor

Dear Mr. Tothemax,

(Amend this paragraph to fit your situation)
I had my earthquake claim inspected by the adjuster on
02-16-199X. I received a check from your office on 02-22-199X
for $X,000.00. The adjuster told me by telephone what I would be
receiving, but made no effort to reach a settlement with me. While
it was very difficult to get a contractor out to inspect my property
after the earthquake, now that I have one, I believe we can
conclude this claim.

I have obtained a contractor's estimate for $XX,000.00 for repairs
to my home. I am requesting a reinspection of the damage to my
home. Please have an adjuster call me first so that I may arrange
for the adjuster to meet with the contractor. Of course I expect
your company will comply with all obligations under the policy
and all time limits required by law.

Sincerely,

Ineeda Moore

Sample Letter To Request A Reinspection Due To The Presence Of New Cracks

XYZ Insurance Company
100 North First Street
Los Angeles, CA. 90000

RE: Insured: Reed Mylyps   Date: 07-24-199X
    Date of Loss: 01-17-199X
    Policy #: 123-35-78 A
    Claim #: 436-85-056

CERTIFIED MAIL, RETURN RECEIPT REQUESTED

Attention: Ms. Key Pitclosed, Catastrophe Supervisor

Dear Ms. Pitclosed,

(Amend the following paragraphs to fit your situation)
I had my earthquake claim inspected by the adjuster on 02-26-199X. I received a check from your office on 03-12-199X for $X,000.00.

I have just recently noticed new cracks in several walls. I am therefore requesting a reinspection of my home. Please have an adjuster call me first so that I may arrange for the adjuster to meet with my contractor.

Of course I expect your company will comply with all obligations under the policy and time limits required by law.

Sincerely,

Reed Mylyps

Sample Letter To Request Contractor's Profit And Overhead

XYZ insurance company
100 North First Street
Los Angeles, CA. 90090

RE: Insured: Iwannit Phair   Date: 05-27-199X
       Date of Loss: 01-17-199X
       Policy #: 133-45-98 A
       Claim #: 454-85-006

CERTIFIED MAIL, RETURN RECEIPT REQUESTED

Attention : Mr. Shortchange, Claims Supervisor

Dear Sir,

(Amend the following paragraph to fit your situation)
I had my earthquake claim inspected by the adjuster on 03-16-199X. I received a check from your office on 04-22-199X for $XX,000.00. The adjuster told me by telephone what I would be receiving without making any effort to reach a settlement with me. I see from the adjuster's estimate that profit and overhead was not included in the estimate. Initially, it was very difficult to get a contractor on short notice. Now that I have one, I believe we can conclude this claim.

I have just recently received a contractor's estimate for $XXX,000.00 for repairs to my home. I am therefore requesting a reinspection of the damage to my home. Please have an adjuster call me first so that I may arrange for the adjuster to meet with the contractor. Of course I expect your company to comply with all obligations under the policy and all time limits required by law.

Sincerely,

Iwannit Phair

Sample Letter To Claim The Unpaid Half Of Your Block Wall Or Fence

XYZ Insurance Company
100 N. First Street
Los Angeles, California 90000

RE: Insured: Itza Mifense   Date: 04-11-199X
       Date of Loss: 01-17-199X
       Policy#: 1290-121212
       Claim#: 123-456-788

CERTIFIED MAIL, RETURN RECEIPT REQUESTED

Attention: Terry Tookhafe, Adjuster

Dear Mr. Tookhafe,

(Amend the following paragraph to fit your situation)
I received a check on 03-23-199X representing payment for my earthquake loss for $XX,000.00. After reviewing the estimate of damage you provided, I noticed I was only paid for half of the full cost to replace my (*block walls or fence*). I have since obtained a contractor's estimate to repair these walls and it is enclosed. I have verified with my neighbor that I am the sole owner of the block walls situated on the west and north sides of my property.

I believe this new information supports an additional claim. Please accept this letter and enclosures as a revised claim. I expect payment in full for the damage to the above property.

Sincerely,

Itza Mifense

CHAPTER 15

THE KILLER DEDUCTIBLE

Is There a Way Around This Killer Deductible?

The answer is no. The insurance policy is a contract. If you purchased it with a deductible, that amount must be subtracted from the claim. This part is etched in stone. BUT—there may be ways to lessen its effect.

YOUR STRATEGY
BE THOROUGH IN IDENTIFYING
ALL YOUR DAMAGE.

The amount you will ultimately receive is based solely on the ability of you and your contractor to accurately point out all your damage. Properly include all areas of damage so the deductible is taken off the *maximum* amount you are entitled to claim. This can result in "covering" your deductible amount quickly. Point out areas of damage that the adjuster should include in the settlement. This is no time to be humble.

Driveways and sidewalks are good places to start. Be honest about old cracks, but point out where the old cracks have expanded or gotten longer or wider because of the earthquake.

Don't forget garage floors. They are part of your garage and frequently are cracked by earthquakes. They are also expensive to replace!

Pictures swing wildly during an earthquake and damage the paint and wallpaper. Falling objects nick kitchen floors. Carpets get filled with glass particles from broken glass. Furniture gets nicked and scratched. Nails in flooring, walls, ceiling and roofs loosen. Paneling pops loose. Windows and door openings are no longer square. The list goes on and on.

The point is to recognize that although the deductible is etched in stone, the dollar value of the damage isn't. THE ADJUSTER MUST CONSIDER YOUR CLAIM FOR REPAIRS OR REPLACEMENT FOR EACH ITEM OF DAMAGE. Follow through with the adjuster to see that each item of damage is accounted for in the final settlement.

How Percentage Deductibles Work

Deductibles of 1%, 5%, 10% or 15% are typical. The deductible is usually based on the amount of insurance you have and *not* on the amount of the loss. However, deductibles are applied differently depending on the type of policy you have.

The Separate Earthquake Policy

With this policy, the percentage deductible is figured on the total amount of your coverage and is subtracted from the total amount of your loss. For example:

> **You purchased a $100,000 coverage earthquake policy with a 10% deductible.**
>
> **Your deductible is 10% of your coverage or $10,000.**
>
> **You have $23,000 in damage.**
>
> **Subtract the deductible of $10,000 from the loss amount of $23,000.**
>
> **You would receive $13,000.**

The "Endorsed On" Earthquake Coverage

With the "endorsed on" earthquake coverage, the percentage deductible is figured for *each item* of coverage and is applied individually. For example:

A sample Homeowners policy with a 10% deductible has the following limits of insurance coverage:

	INSURANCE	DEDUCTIBLE
Home	$100,000	$ 10,000
Other Structures	$ 10,000	$ 1,000
Personal Property	$ 80,000	$ 8,000
Additional Living Expense	$ 30,000	$ -0-*

*(the deductible does not apply to this coverage)

158

THE APPENDIX

DIRECTORY OF THE STATE INSURANCE DEPARTMENTS

ALABAMA
Alabama Insurance Dept.
135 South Union Street
Montgomery, Al 36130-3401
(205) 269-3550

ALASKA
Alaska Insurance Dept.
800 East Diamond, Suite 560
Anchorage, AK 99515
(907) 349-1230

ARIZONA
Arizona Insurance Dept.
Consumer Affairs Division
3030 N. 3RD ST. Suite 1100
Phoenix, AZ 85012
(602) 255-4783

ARKANSAS
Arkansas Insurance Dept.
Consumer Service Division
400 University Tower Building
University and 12TH Street
Little Rock, AR 72204
(501) 686-2945

CALIFORNIA
California Insurance Department
Consumer Services Division
Claims Service Bureau
3450 Wilshire Blvd.
Los Angeles, CA 90010
(800) 927-4357 (in state)

COLORADO
Colorado Division of Insurance
1560 Broadway, Suite 850
Denver, CO 80202
(303) 894-7499

CONNECTICUT
Connecticut Insurance Department
P. O. Box 816
Hartford, CT 06142-0816
(203) 297-3800

DELAWARE
Delaware Insurance Department
841 Silver Lake Blvd.
Dover, DE 19901
(302) 739-4251

DISTRICT OF COLUMBIA
District of Columbia
Insurance Department
613 G Street, NW; Room 619
P. O. Box 37200
Washington, DC 20013-7200
(202) 727-8017

FLORIDA
Florida Department of Insurance
State Capitol; Plaza Level Eleven
200 East Gaines Street
Tallahassee, Fl 32399-0300
(800) 342-2762 (in state)
(904) 922-3100

GEORGIA
Georgia Insurance Department
2 Martin Luther King, Jr. Drive
Room 716, West tower
Atlanta, GA 30334
(404) 656-2056

HAWAII
Hawaii Department of Commerce and
Consumer Affairs
Insurance Division
P. O. Box 3614
Honolulu, HI 96811-3614
(808) 586-2790

IDAHO
Idaho Insurance Dept.
Public service department
500 South 10TH Street
Boise, ID 83720
(208) 334-4250

ILLINOIS
Illinois Insurance Dept.
320 West Washington Street
4TH Floor
Springfield, IL 62767
(217) 782-4515

INDIANA
Indiana Insurance Dept.
311 West Washington Street
Suite 300
Indianapolis, IN 46204
(317) 232-2395

IOWA
Iowa Insurance Division
Lucas State Office Building
East 12TH and Grand Streets
Des Moines, IA 50319
(515) 281-5705

KANSAS
Kansas Insurance Dept.
420 Southwest 9TH Street
Topeka, KS 66612-1678
(913) 296-3071

KENTUCKY
Kentucky Insurance Dept.
229 West Main Street
P. O. Box 517
Frankfort, KY 40602
(502) 564-3630

LOUISIANA
Louisiana Insurance Dept.
P. O. Box 94214
Baton Rouge, LA 70804-9214
(504) 342-5900

MAINE
Maine Bureau of Insurance
Consumer Division
State House, Station 34
Augusta, ME 04333
(207) 582-8707

MARYLAND
Maryland Insurance Dept.
Complaints and Investigation Unit
501 St. Paul Place
Baltimore, MD 21202-2272
(410) 333-6300

MASSACHUSETTS
Massachusetts Insurance Dept.
Consumer Services Section
280 Friend Street
Boston, MA 02114
(617) 727-7189

MICHIGAN
Michigan Insurance Dept.
P.O. Box 30220
Lansing, MI 48909
(517) 373-0220

MINNESOTA
Minnesota Insurance Dept.
Department of Commerce
133 East 7TH Street
St. Paul, MN 55101
(612) 296-4026

MISSISSIPPI
Mississippi Insurance Dept.
Consumer Assistance Division
P.O. Box 79
Jackson, MS 39205
(601) 359-3569

MISSOURI
Missouri Division of Insurance
Consumer Services Section
P. O. Box 690
Jefferson City, MO 65102-0690
(314) 751-2640

MONTANA
Montana Insurance Dept.
126 North Sanders, Room 270
P.O. Box 4009
Helena, MT 59604
(800) 332-6148 (in state)
(406) 444-2040

NEBRASKA
Nebraska Insurance Dept.
Terminal Building
941 O Street, Suite 400
Lincoln, NE 68508
(402) 471-2201

NEVADA
Nevada Department of Commerce
Insurance Division, Consumer Sect.
1665 Hot Springs Road
Capitol Complex, Suite 152
Carson City, NV 89701
(702) 687-4270

NEW HAMPSHIRE
New Hampshire Insurance Dept.
Property and Casualty Division
169 Manchester Street
Concord, NH 03301-5151
(603) 271-2261

NEW JERSEY
New Jersey Insurance Dept.
20 West State Street
Roebling Building
Trenton, NJ 08625-0325
(609) 292-4757

NEW MEXICO
New Mexico Insurance Dept.
P. O. Drawer 1269
Sante Fe, NM 87504-1269
(505) 827-4500

NEW YORK
New York Insurance Dept.
160 West Broadway
New York, NY 10013
(212) 602-0203 (NYC)
(800) 342-3736 (in state, outside NYC)

NORTH CAROLINA
North Carolina Insurance Dept.
Consumer Services
P.O. Box 26387
Raleigh, NC 27611
(919) 733-2004

NORTH DAKOTA
North Dakota Insurance Dept.
Capitol Building, 5TH Floor
600 East Boulevard Ave.
Bismark, ND 58505-0320
(701) 224-2440

OHIO
Ohio Insurance Dept.
Consumer Services Division
2100 Stella Court
Columbus, OH 43266-0566
(614) 644-2673

OKLAHOMA
Oklahoma Insurance Dept.
P.O. Box 53408
Oklahoma City, OK 73152-3408
(405) 521-2828

OREGON
Oregon Department of Insurance
Insurance Div. / Consumer Advocate
440-7 Labor and Industry Building
Salem, OR 97310
(503) 378-4484

PENNSYLVANIA
Pennsylvania Insurance Department
1321 Strawberry Square
Harrisburg, PA 17120
(717) 787-2317

RHODE ISLAND
Rhode Island Insurance Division
233 Richmond Street, Suite 233
Providence,RI 02903-4233
(401) 277-2223

SOUTH CAROLINA
South Carolina Insurance Department
P.O. Box 100105
Columbia, SC 29202-3105
(803) 737-6140

SOUTH DAKOTA
South Dakota Insurance department
Consumer Assistance Section
500 East Central
Pierre, SD 57501-3940
(605) 773-3563

TENNESSEE
Tennessee Department
of Commerce and Insurance
Policyholders Service Section
500 James Robertson Parkway
4TH Floor
Nashville, TN 37243-0582
(800) 342-4029 (in state)
(615) 741-4955

TEXAS
Texas Board of Insurance
Complaints Division
1110 San Jacinto Blvd.
Austin, TX 78701-1998
(512) 463-6501

UTAH
Utah Insurance Dept.
Consumer Services
3110 State Office Building
Salt Lake City, UT 84114
(801) 530-6400

VERMONT
Vermont Department of Insurance and
Banking
Consumer Complaint Division
120 State Street
Montpelier, VT 05602
(802) 828-3301

VIRGINIA
Virginia Insurance Department
Consumer Services Division
700 Jefferson Building
P. O. Box 1157
Richmond, VA 23209
(804) 786-7691

WASHINGTON
Washington Insurance Dept.
Insurance Building
P. O. Box 40255
Olympia, WA 98504-0255
(800) 562-6900 (in state)
(206) 753-7300

WEST VIRGINIA
West Virginia Insurance Dept.
P. O. Box 50540
2019 Washington Street, East
Charleston, WV 25305-0540
(304) 558-3386

WISCONSIN
Wisconsin Insurance Dept.
Complaints Department
P. O. Box 7873
Madison, WI 53707
(608) 266-0103

WYOMING
Wyoming Insurance Dept.
Herschler Building
122 West 25TH Street
Cheyenne, WY 82002
(307) 777-7401

GLOSSARY

Actual Cash Value or "A.C.V." — Full replacement cost less depreciation.

Additional Living Expense —This is also known as A.L.E. or Loss of Use. It is additional expenses beyond what you would normally spend living at home.

Adjuster — A person who investigates and settles insurance claims.

> *Staff*--employee of the insurance company's claim department.
>
> *Independent*--a person who charges a fee to an insurance company to adjust the company's claims.
>
> *Public*--a person hired by you to settle the claim with the insurance company on your behalf.

Advance Payment — Funds provided to you to pay for immediate needs, to be deducted from the final settlement.

Agent — A person who sells the products of the insurance company. The person responsible for your insurance coverage needs.

Ambiguities — Used interchangeably with "grey area." These are parts or words of the policy that mean more than one thing or may be unclear.

Appearance Allowance — An argument used by adjusters to explain paying less than the full value of a repair or replacement because there is still some functional use of the property that is damaged.

Appraisal Clause — The way the policy provides to resolve disagreements over amounts and extent or scope of damage to property.

Bad Faith — These two words identify wrongdoing by the insurance company when the company fails to treat you fairly and in good faith.

Burden of Proof — The responsibility of one party to produce evidence to support his position.

Business Interruption — Coverage for lost income when the business is unable to continue operations because of damage by a covered peril.

By-Laws — Rules or regulations adopted by a condominium association.

Cash Out — An amount of money in lieu of the cost to properly repair or replace an item.

Conditions — A qualification, limitation, or obligation of a party to the insurance contract.

Contiguous — Adjoining or in close proximity.

Cosmetic Damage — A term explaining damage that does not effect the functional usage or structural stability of the property. Superficial damage.

Debris Removal Clauses — Additional coverage to pay for debris that must be removed but is not part of the repair process for damage to your property.

Declarations Page — The first page to an insurance policy that identifies the insured, the property insured, the address of the property, the agent, the amount of coverage, the coverage forms, and when coverage takes effect.

Deductible — A clause in the policy stating the amount of the loss you must absorb.

Depreciation — The loss in value of property due to age, use or obsolescence.

Duties of insured after loss — Your obligations under the policy that you must perform prior to the insurance company fulfilling its promise to pay.

Exclusions — Usually a laundry list of things that can damage your property but are not covered by the policy.

F.E.M.A. — Federal Emergency Management Agency.

Fraud — Knowingly presenting false or fraudulent claims to the insurance company (*knowingly means consciously and intentionally*).

Good Faith — Honesty of purpose and freedom from intention to defraud by either you or the insurance company.

Grey Areas — *(see ambiguity)*

Holdback Depreciation — The amount of money representing the depreciation of your property that is withheld from your initial settlement until the repairs of the damage are complete or the items are replaced.

Homeowners Policy — A package insurance policy with property and liability coverages.

> *HO-3 form*--this is the most common type of Homeowners policy. It provides all risk coverage for the dwelling and other structures and named perils for personal property.

Late Claim — Filing a claim beyond a reasonable amount of time after the damage occurred.

Legal Department — A division within most insurance companies where coverage questions and coverage denials are reviewed.

Lien Waivers — A waiver of a subcontractor's or material supplier's right to make a claim against your property to secure payment for a debt.

Like Kind and Quality — The same kind and quality of product or as close to the same kind and quality of product that can be obtained to replace the property that was damaged or destroyed.

Local Building Codes — Building construction standards for safety set by local governmental authorities.

Negotiation — A process of communication between two parties to agree on the terms and conditions of a settlement.

Other Structures — Buildings or structures on your property, that are not attached to your home.

Overhead (*and profit*) — These terms are usually used together to represent the expenses and profit of a general contractor. Insurance companies try to limit these two items to 20% of the total cost of the repair job.

Partial Payment — A payment for the agreed amount of the claim with the understanding it is only partial satisfaction of the claim.

Personal Property — Insurance lingo for anything you own that is not a structure or a building.

Power Surge — A spike or jump of electricity that may damage your personal property.

Price Guide — The list of prices an adjuster uses to write estimates.

Promissory Note — A signed document promising to pay another a specified amount of money.

Proof of Claim — Insurance words having a special meaning in California. When you state you are submitting your Proof of Claim, the adjuster must respond to your claim by a certain time. (See the state time limits in the chapter, "Hardball Negotiation Strategies.")

Proof of Loss — Insurance words that have two meanings, generally the form (provided by the adjuster) you sign and submit for payment of your claim. It can also mean your documents that support your claim (such as estimates or receipts).

Recorded Statement — Questions asked by the adjuster over the phone or in person, recorded on tape. It preserves information regarding the claim.

Replacement Cost — Today's cost to replace an item with "Like kind and Quality."

Replacement Cost Coverage — Insurance coverage which provides the total cost to replace the property with no deduction for depreciation.

Salvage — The useful portion of the property which remains after it has been damaged.

Scope of Repair — The extent of damage or type of repairs needed due to the disaster.

Settlement — An agreement between the insured and the insurance company on the amount to pay for the claim.

Stated Value — See Valued Policy Provision.

Statement Under Oath — Also referred to as an Examination Under Oath. A series of questions put to the insured, under oath, in front of a court reporter.

Supplemental Claim — An additional claim made after payment has already been made on the same claim.

Temporary Repairs — Any reasonable repair which protects the property from further damage.

Total Loss —

      Constructive, the cost to repair exceeds the value.

      Obvious, obviously cannot be repaired.

Unfair Claim Practices Act — This is the generic term for the set of laws of each state that say an insurance company must fulfill its promises to the policyholder according to certain rules. These rules set the minimum standard of conduct.

Valued Policy Provisions — A policy provision required by state law which requires the insurance company, in the event the home is a total loss, to pay the full amount for which the home is insured.

INDEX

NOTES

NOTES

NOTES

Notes from the Author

After numerous requests for help and advice on insurance claims, I recognized an enormous need for a source of information. The first publications of their kind, the **GUNN GUIDES** are written with righteous indignation for all those people who have nowhere to go for help on their insurance claims and may suffer financially as a result.

To continue to provide useful and current information, I need your help. Tell me your experiences. Tell me what was helpful in the book and where the book can be improved.

I am also searching for good photographs of damage caused by disasters to be used in future editions of the **GUNN GUIDES**. If you have any interesting or unique photographs you would like to donate and share with the public, please send them. Include the negatives and write a short paragraph explaining the photos, and give me permission to use them. (Sorry, negatives and photographs cannot not be returned.)

I hope my work has been of service to you. I try to make myself available to the public for assistance in major catastrophes. Maybe our paths will cross.

Very sincerely,

Travis

THE
CLAIM SIMPLI-FILER
DISASTER PACK
Includes:

- **A complete filing system and personal record keeper for documenting the events of your claim**

- **A "To Do"checklist**

- **Your labor and expenses itemizer**

- **Advance payment forms**

- **The Total Recall Property Inventory List**

- **Personal property inventory forms**

- **Spoiled food inventory forms**

- **Additional Living Expense forms**

- **A guide to recording a conversation**

- **Photograph mounting sheets**

- **Claim payment summary**

- **All of the forms included throughout the book**

- **Additional resources available to you**

- **Updates specific to your disaster and state**

- **And much more!**

ALL FOR ONLY $26.95 ORDER NOW!

Order Form

☎ **Telephone Orders: Call Toll Free: 1 (800) 98-T-GUNN.**
   Have your credit card ready.

〰 **Fax Orders: (719) 481-0027**

✉ **Postal Orders: CrossFire Publishing, GUNN GUIDES,**
   P.O. Box 1209, Monument, C0 80132

Please send the following **GUNN GUIDE** books or materials. I understand
that I may return any books—for any reason, no questions asked—for a full
refund (receipt must be included).

❑ 📁 **THE CLAIM SIMPLI-FILER $26.95**
   Please circle type of claim: EARTHQUAKE   HURRICANE
                                   TORNADO   WIND   HAIL

❑ 📖 EARTHQUAKE CLAIMS: **TRADE SECRETS YOU MUST**
   KNOW $26.95

❑ 📖 TORNADO, WIND AND HAIL CLAIMS: **TRADE**
   SECRETS YOU MUST KNOW $26.95

❑ 📖 HURRICANE CLAIMS: **TRADE SECRETS YOU MUST**
   KNOW $26.95

Name:_____   _____

Street Address:_____

City:_____State:_____Zip:_____

Phone: (   )_____

Sales Tax: Please add 8.25% for books shipped to Texas or 7.25% to Colorado
          addresses

Shipping and Handling: Priority air mail: $3.50 Overnight: $15.00

Payment: ❑Check or Money Order
         ❑Credit card: ❑Visa ❑MasterCard ❑AMEX ❑Discover

Card number:_____

Name on card:_____Exp. date:____/____

Call *Toll Free* and Order Now